Maryann
5
68 No. ~~~~~~~, 1
Pittsford, NY 14534
thebackyardshawoman
@gmail.com

BONE BROTH

BONE BROTH

101 Essential Recipes and Age-Old Remedies to Heal Your Body

QUINN FARRAR WILSON

SONOMA
PRESS

For my darling grandfather Pak
and my wonderful grandmother Beep,
with special thanks to my family.
Hubba hubba.

With Love, Ulo Ulo

CONTENTS

INTRODUCTION

One spring morning in San Diego, where I live, a friend dropped over to brief me on his recent trip to a conference about one of our shared interests—traditional foods.

"You're not going to believe this," he said. "Instead of coffee in the morning, they served bone broth."

A cup of bone broth first thing in the morning? It sounded strange to me at first. But the more I thought about it, the more I was intrigued.

Several years earlier, after spending a couple of years working for an organic farm, I'd become involved in my community's locally produced–foods movement. I had purged my kitchen and pantry of any and all processed food products. So, with my culinary background, I reasoned, why couldn't I make my own broth? How hard could it be?

I did my research, picked up an order of bones from a local sustainable farm, rolled up my sleeves, and reached for the pre–Civil War cast-iron cauldron that had belonged to my great-great-grandmother. What better way to resurrect a traditional food than by using this antique vessel I'd spent months restoring?

I browned the bones, chopped my vegetables, added vinegar, allowed the mixture to sit for the time needed to draw out the minerals, fired-up my stove top, and kept my eyes practically glued to that bubbling cauldron for the next 36 hours. At the end of that time, I had two questions: *Is broth supposed to be black? Is broth supposed to taste like the bottom of a barbecue pit?* I didn't think so, but what did I know?

I poured the precious black liquid into mason jars and let it cool overnight. In the morning I skimmed off the fat, took a sip of my very first bone broth, and promptly tossed out the whole batch.

I love sharing the story of my failed first batch because it illustrates something you need to know about making bone broth: Failure is definitely an option, so you're going to need some perseverance, since it's all about trial and error in the beginning. That's because every kitchen is different, so the process involves many unknown variables, and problems don't always have precise solutions.

But you also need to know that making bone broth at home is easy if you have the right tools and just a little patience. When you make your own broth, you're free to please your own palate. You'll always have broth on hand when you need it, and in the long run that saves you time and money.

But back to my own trials and errors. I kept experimenting. I exchanged the romance of my great-great-grandmother's cauldron (and the hazards of a 36-hour open flame on my stove top) for a $3 slow cooker from the thrift store. I continued to learn from my mistakes. It took me a few tries, but I was finally able to make a great bone broth. And once I could actually drink my own broth, I started enjoying a hot mug of it four mornings a week. Why only four? Because that was the exact number of mason jars my little cooker yielded!

Even that amount of bone broth was enough to bring about dramatic changes in my health. It's not that I had been harboring great expectations. I wasn't sick, and I wasn't trying to treat any particular ailment. I had my issues, of course, like most people do—a sensitive and erratic stomach, skin that didn't do well in the heat, and constant, excruciating bone pain from 20 years of dental implants and experimental surgeries that I'd endured since the age of 10, when a skiing accident knocked my front teeth out. All the same, making bone broth was purely experimental for me.

But even though I wasn't looking for miracle cures, it took only two weeks of this modest bone broth regimen for the skin on my hands to become sleek and supple, and my complexion start to glow. After six weeks, the healing really kicked in—one day my bone pain just stopped, and my bone tissue has remained strong, healthy, and dense ever since. After six months of bone broth, my stomach issues also began to improve, and after eight months they were completely resolved.

Little did I dream, after that initial fiasco in my kitchen, that I would one day own and operate a bone broth business! Balanced and Bright Bone Broth is now so successful that I usually don't make bone broth at home these days, though I still enjoy the ritual of a hot mug of broth in the morning. I usually season it with cinnamon, sugar, and a pat of butter, but it's versatile enough for a sprinkle of salt and a squeeze of lemon instead. It shines at dinnertime, too, since it slips beautifully into so many recipes.

And I certainly never imagined that I would one day write this book to help you bring the benefits of bone broth into your life! In these pages, you'll learn everything you need to know about equipment, ingredients, and cooking methods. The book not only includes plenty of recipes for farmers' market–quality bone broth you can make at home, but it also gives you lots of ideas for incorporating bone broth into your diet.

There are many routes to developing an interest in bone broth, but they all lead to better health and increased wellness. Whatever your reason for beginning this journey, you've taken the first step. Thank you for letting me walk beside you.

CHAPTER 1

THE NOURISHING CUP

Welcome to my world—the world of bone broth! I'll be teaching you how to make different varieties of broth, covering all of the basics as well as a few more adventurous undertakings. I'll share all my homemade broth secrets to ensure wonderful results, and I'll give you plenty of ideas for getting more bone broth into your diet.

In this chapter, we'll explore the roots and the modern renaissance of this ancient remedial go-to. We'll take a look at bone broth's nutritional components and health benefits, and we'll consider what's involved in making bone broth, not just as a soothing hot drink but as a transformative lifestyle choice.

A Traditional Cure-All

The roots of bone broth are truly ancient. By the early Stone Age, some of our human ancestors had learned to use fire and rudimentary tools like knives and arrowheads, and with agriculture still in the future, animals were these early humans' main source of food. Our very earliest ancestors probably didn't make bone broth, and yet it seems that they understood the nutritional value of bone marrow, as the smashed animal bones found at archaeological sites suggest.

We may never know exactly when animal bones were first brought to a boil and simmered with vegetables to produce a savory broth, but there's no denying that bone broth eventually became a culinary staple of all human cultures around the world, rich or poor, sedentary or nomadic. And bone broth remains an ingredient prized by most chefs because they know that its complexity and richness will enhance almost any dish.

In the early days of the United States, as in virtually every other part of the world, bone broth was recognized as a soothing, restorative, healing food. That emphasis had really taken hold by the nineteenth century, when bone broth was called "beef tea" or "invalid beef tea" and had come to be seen mainly as a beverage for sick people. It was produced in home kitchens and also in hospitals.

In the early decades of twentieth century America, there were still plenty of farmers and small farms, and varieties of bone broth continued to be made in most households. By this time, though, bone broth was also served with most meals. It was valued for its nutritional properties and for the well-being of people who were not sick. With farmers raising and slaughtering their own animals, and with cooks in farm kitchens practicing nose-to-tail use of every last bit of a carcass, it's no wonder that bone broth was so often on the menu.

But some 30 years later, with the end of World War II, suburbs and highways replaced many small farms, and food production became an arena for industrialization. As one result of that trend, true-to-form traditional bone broth mostly disappeared from American home kitchens.

BROTH VS. STOCK: WHAT'S THE DIFFERENCE?

You say "stock," I say "broth"—let's call the whole thing off. Or not!

Discussions of whether broth should be called "stock" or stock should be called "broth" can become quite heated (pun fully intended). But there's no need to argue, since there's no real difference between the two.

Which is not to say that a few distinctions can't be made.

The word *stock,* meaning the liquid created when meat or vegetables are boiled in water, dates from 1764 and is probably related to the Middle English word *stok*, which came to mean a supply of something kept on hand for future use.

By contrast, the word *broth* can be traced to an Old High German verb root, *bhreue-*, which in conjugated form denoted the acts of heating, boiling, and bubbling. And when that verb root evolved into a noun, it meant the liquid in which something had heated, boiled, and bubbled.

But forget about the past. The culinary dictionary at the popular website What's Cooking America defines broth as "a flavorful liquid resulting from the long simmering of meat, vegetables, poultry, or fish," and notes that broth is "also known as stock." Then, just to rub it in, this dictionary doesn't even include an entry for *stock*.

So, let's disagree, if we must, about to-MAY-to and to-MAH-to, but let's agree that *broth* and *stock*, regardless of linguistic pedigree, are both names for a nutritious, savory, traditional food that can be enjoyed on its own or kept on hand as the base for soups, stews, sauces, and other delectable creations.

Today, most North Americans and other Westerners see broth as the product of a bouillon cube added to hot water, or as a shelf-stable canned or boxed liquid. But such so-called broth is low in nutritional value. It offers little more than convenience spiced up with artificial flavors.

Things are different in East Asia, where bone broth has been used as medicine for centuries. Even today, practitioners of Eastern medicine continue to swear by bone broth's healing properties. They see it as promoting strength, building red blood cells, and enhancing kidney and liver function, and they use medicinal herbs to bolster its effects.

Here in the West, people are rediscovering bone broth for all kinds of reasons. Some adopt the Paleo diet and then come to recognize the role that bone broth can play in this way of eating. Others, like me, find bone broth while pursuing an interest in traditional foods. And still others learn about bone broth and its benefits when they decide to give up processed junk for good old-fashioned real nutrition.

But bone broth is more than a trend or the superfood du jour. In fact, lots of people have learned about bone broth when it was recommended for them by professional wellness advocates. Nutritionists, acupuncturists, naturopathic physicians, and other alternative health-care providers routinely suggest bone broth for the following purposes:

- Repair of joints and bone tissue
- Improvement of hair, skin, and nails
- Alleviation of acne
- Promotion of fertility
- Wellness support during pregnancy
- Strengthening before surgery
- Postsurgical healing
- Healing of traumatic injuries and wounds
- Symptom relief for autoimmune disorders like rheumatoid arthritis and Crohn's disease
- Palliative and hospice care

With the list of bone broth's healing properties long and varied, today people are rediscovering stock as a versatile source of nourishment, paving the way for a modern broth renaissance.

Bone Broth Deconstructed

Bone broth presents a paradox: It's one of the world's most ancient and familiar foods, but its reputed effects on the body remain somewhat mysterious. That's because we're still waiting for scientific evidence of how bone broth works, and for scientific confirmation of bone broth's long-term benefits.

Why have so many people, for so many centuries, seen bone broth as a vehicle of healing and wellness? Maybe some empirical answers will come as medical schools place more emphasis on nutritional education, and as academic scientists conduct more nutritional studies and publish their results in respected peer-reviewed journals. For now, let's peek under the hood of this nutritional powerhouse and take a look at its components.

CARTILAGE, which also goes by the less attractive name *gristle*, is rich not just in collagen but also in chondroitin sulfate, elastin,

BONE BROTH AND THE GUT

It's not surprising that the human digestive system is often vulnerable to disorders. In an adult, the small intestine alone is about 22 feet long, with a surface area of about 323 square feet. That's a lot of real estate—and we're not just talking about a long, smooth tube. It's a twisting landscape of peaks and valleys filled with microscopic fingerlike structures called *villi* that help the body digest food and absorb nutrients.

 Many of us, as modern Westerners, have spent years consuming artificial chemicals in processed foods. And for some of us, the chemicals in processed foods are suspected of having consequences—sometimes subtle, sometimes severe—tied to acute or chronic ailments. As one consequence of a highly processed diet, the gut may become depleted of the elements it needs for healthy functioning. Then, when symptoms appear, the conditioned response is to run to the doctor for medications that mask the problem or, worse, cause their own side effects.

What many modern Westerners don't know is that digestive symptoms can be relieved and even eliminated by a simple change of diet. Maybe the small intestine's sensitivity and the healing effects of dietary change are both due to the digestive system's massive amount of GALT, or gut-associated lymphoid tissue, which normally constitutes the immune system's first line of defense. Nobody really knows, because the healing mechanism behind dietary change is not well understood. Nutritionists often cite a change in diet as the solution to a condition known as *leaky gut syndrome*, but most physicians deny that such a syndrome exists.

Whatever the scientific verdict turns out to be, the anecdotal evidence is in: I'm taking my place as exhibit A, and I'm here to tell you that bone broth is a gut-friendly, gut-soothing, gut-healing food that completely cured my digestive problems in a matter of months.

and glucose. The cartilage in bone broth is believed to promote skin and joint health and to benefit people who suffer from osteopenia as well as from the osteoporosis and osteoarthritis that can follow.

COLLAGEN AND GELATIN are similar. The major difference is that collagen exists naturally inside a living organism, and gelatin is what collagen becomes after it's extracted from that organism. Collagen controls many cellular functions and is the major protein found in the extracellular matrix, which is the name for those molecules that are secreted by cells and then act as a structural and biochemical scaffold for surrounding cells. The collagen and gelatin in bone broth are believed to promote healing of wounds and soft tissue and to support the formation and repair of cartilage and bone tissue.

BONE MARROW contains myeloid lymphoid cells, the building blocks of the body's red and white blood cells. It also contains healthy saturated fats. Bone marrow is believed to strengthen the immune system, aid in blood clotting, and provide oxygen to cells. It's also said to ease digestion and to relieve the inflammation that accompanies irritable bowel syndrome (IBS), gluten sensitivity or intolerance, and celiac disease. These are just a few of the reasons why bone marrow is sometimes referred to as a global wellness tool. It can be consumed as one element of a long-cooked broth or eaten straight from the bone as a delicacy.

AMINO ACIDS, a major component of protein, are the crucial building blocks of the body's tissues. Two of the most essential amino acids are *glycine*, which promotes oxygenation of the blood, and *proline*, which is necessary for the production of collagen; both glycine and proline are also needed for wound healing. Not all the essential amino acids are produced or stored in the body, so they have to be obtained through food, specifically through sources of protein, including bone broth. Because it contains an abundance of amino acids, bone broth is believed to promote the body's immunity and antioxidant activity, enhance muscle development, and help regulate the functions of the central nervous system.

NATURE'S BOTOX

There is no denying a good bone broth does wonders for your skin—I can account firsthand for that. Around the age of 30, our bodies start to lose their natural levels of collagen, thus beginning the process of aging. Drinking bone broth, however, helps your body keep up those declining collagen levels. Containing key elements like collagen, gelatin, glycine, and proline, bone broth supplements your skin with everything it needs to stay glowing and healthy, both inside and out.

MINERALS are necessary for the development of connective tissue and bone, and they play a role in supporting the functions of the nervous system. Because bone broth contains calcium, silicon, sulfur, magnesium, and phosphorous in addition to a number of trace minerals, it is believed to help repair nerve damage, such as the kind that occurs during surgery or may result from an accident.

Bone Broth as a Lifestyle Choice

Bone broth is a nourishing traditional food, and drinking it first thing in the morning is a delicious way to greet the day. These two facts are undeniable.

But if you're turning to bone broth as a remedy for one or more conditions, you'll probably find that just a little patience is everything. Although you may see a few unexpected improvements almost right away, as I did when I noticed my skin softening after only two weeks, chances are you'll wait longer than that for major results—remember, I drank bone broth four times a week for eight months before my stomach finally settled down.

And while bone broth is many things, it isn't a magic bullet. I hope and expect that drinking bone broth and incorporating more bone broth into your daily meals will be a healing experience for you, but healing doesn't necessarily lead to a cure.

Something else to keep in mind is that making and consuming bone broth is just one element of a healthy lifestyle. Even if drinking a cup of bone broth enhances your body's ability to absorb and assimilate vital minerals and other nutrients, that cup of bone broth still won't cancel out junk food, sugary beverages, or artificially sweetened diet sodas (that may be putting you at risk for osteoporosis while you think you're doing yourself a favor because they're sugar-free).

Making bone broth a lifestyle choice means developing your consciousness about all the food you're putting into your body. That's why drinking bone broth goes hand in hand with choosing to adopt a diet of real food and traditional food.

It's never too soon or too late to make that choice, so why not start today? Go through your refrigerator and your pantry, and throw out anything with a label that includes even a single word you can't pronounce. Toss anything that contains high-fructose corn syrup. Lose the tub or stick of margarine, can the can of vegetable shortening, and pour out any cooking oil that's partially hydrogenated. In fact, I think you should stop using cooking oils of any kind, even olive oil (for cooking) and all the other vegetable oils that are believed to be so healthy. I left vegetable oils behind because they're often highly processed even when they're said to be "natural," and because I didn't like what I was hearing about free radicals, highly destructive atoms that may be present in vegetable oils and that can damage the cells.

When the time comes to replace the items you've thrown out, make good choices for yourself:

VEGETABLES. You've probably guessed that I want you to eat lots more vegetables from now on. Consider spending a little more, if you have to, to go organic. After all, you're worth the investment! But your organic veggies may not even be more expensive than the conventionally grown kind if you buy them at your local farmers' market or through a community-supported agriculture (CSA) network.

BREAD. If you eat bread, skip the devitalized, chemical-laden, denatured white variety. Buy bread made from whole grains, or experiment with sourdough and other types of fermented breads. But if you have gluten sensitivity or celiac disease, be skeptical of media or online reports that fermented sourdough bread is safe for you. Those reports are based on a single study from 2011 that had too few participants for a scientific conclusion to be reached. The study's results were far from clear, and you have a lot to lose by swallowing them whole.

MEAT. Since you're reading a book about bone broth, it's fair to assume that you're a carnivore at least some of the time. As for me, I'm with the Temptations—I ain't too proud to beg, and I'm down on my knees right now, pleading with you not to buy meat at your friendly neighborhood corporate supermarket. The meat sold there may be attractively packaged in shiny plastic wrap, but it's rarely from local sources, and it's usually contaminated with antibiotics and the other drugs that go into confining a beautiful animal in an overcrowded, filthy, traumatizing, brutalizing

LARD: THE MISUNDERSTOOD FAT

Lard has a pretty bad reputation, but if you ask yourself why, you probably don't have a clear answer. We've been conditioned to believe that lard is the worst of the worst when it comes to fats, but the truth is that it doesn't deserve its tainted reputation. I cook with lard myself, and many of the recipes in this book include lard as a cooking fat option. While it may be unfamiliar, I'm here to tell you that it's nothing to fear.

In the nineteenth and early twentieth centuries, lard was the most popular cooking fat in the United States. Since the introduction of refined vegetable oils in the early twentieth century, natural fats like lard have fallen out of fashion, being incorrectly linked to obesity. In actuality, lard contains high amounts of vitamin D and more monounsaturated fats than butter. And because it is naturally hydrogenated, it contains no trans fats, unlike the refined vegetable oils that replaced it. Pastured lard has a clean taste and a high smoke point. It is heart healthy, inexpensive, and easy to find at your local sustainable butcher shop, or online. If the idea of cooking with lard irks you, use one of the other options for cooking fat provided in the recipe list. But I'd encourage you to step outside your comfort zone and give it a try.

environment. Don't support that! Adopt a farmer. Befriend a hunter. Or use a vendor who can ship high-quality meat right to your door (see Resources, page 200). Do whatever you can to get as close as possible to the source of your meat.

Bone Broth for Mothers and Infants

Bone broth can alleviate the nausea and joint pain that often accompany pregnancy, and it can protect against loss of bone density. It also passes on nutrients that a baby-to-be can't do without. But remember that you're eating for two, and should consult with a doctor to ensure that adding bone broth to your diet is healthy for you. Be sure that the broth is low in sodium and that it contains only safe levels of every other ingredient you'll be sharing, especially if you're already taking prenatal vitamins.

Once your newborn has reached the age of three to four months, check with your pediatrician to see if there's any reason not to start including bone broth in the baby's diet. If you're given the green light, bone broth can be one of the best and most nourishing foods your baby will consume in the first year of

life. The gelatin in bone broth helps in joint formation. Along with collagen, gelatin also promotes proper development of the digestive tract, and the minerals in broth aid in bone development.

You can add bone broth to almost anything your baby eats or drinks. For example, when you're making a purée, you can use bone broth in place of water, breast milk, or formula. Just be sure the broth has a neutral flavor—and, again, keep the sodium content low, and use only safe levels of non-water-soluble vitamins.

Here are two simple recipes for purées containing bone broth:

Apple and Pear Purée

YIELD: 2 cups
PREP: 10 minutes
COOK: 30 minutes

This is a simple and tasty purée that is great as a first food. Cooking the apples and pears in bone broth provides an extra dose of nutrition. You can keep this purée in the refrigerator for 4 to 5 days, or freeze it in individual storage containers and use as needed.

2 apples, peeled, cored, and sliced
2 pears, peeled, cored, and sliced
2 cups neutral bone broth of your choice
  (page 38)
Dash ground cinnamon

1. Put the apples and pears in a medium saucepan and add the bone broth.

2. Bring to a simmer over medium heat and allow the apples and pears to cook until completely soft, 20 to 25 minutes.

3. Using a slotted spoon, transfer the apples and pears to a food processor. Reserve ½ cup of the bone broth cooking liquid for the purée.

4. Add the cinnamon to the food processor and pulse the apples and pears until they are almost completely smooth. Gradually add the reserved cooking liquid through the feed tube and pulse to combine until you reach your desired consistency.

5. Allow the purée to cool completely before serving.

Sweet Potato Purée

YIELD: 2 cups
PREP: 10 minutes
COOK: 30 minutes

Rich and filling, this recipe will be a hit with your baby. You can continue to cook this recipe as your baby grows, without having to purée it. Simply cut up the cooked discs into toddler-size bites. You can keep this purée in the refrigerator for 4 to 5 days, or freeze it in individual storage containers and use as needed.

2 medium sweet potatoes, peeled and cut into
  ½-inch-thick discs
2 cups neutral bone broth of your choice
  (page 38)
⅛ teaspoon ground nutmeg

1. Put the sweet potatoes in a large saucepan and add the bone broth.

2. Bring to a simmer over medium heat and allow the sweet potatoes to cook until completely soft, 20 to 25 minutes.

3. Using a slotted spoon, transfer the sweet potatoes to a food processor. Reserve ½ cup of the bone broth cooking liquid for the purée.

4. Add the nutmeg to the food processor and pulse the sweet potatoes until they are almost smooth. Gradually add the reserved cooking liquid through the feed tube and pulse to combine until you reach your desired consistency.

5. Allow the purée to cool completely before serving.

CHAPTER 2

IN THE KITCHEN

N ow that you're acquainted with the history, nature, and benefits of bone broth, let's hit the kitchen! In this chapter, we'll talk about choosing the best bones and other ingredients. Then we'll cover the basics of cooking, including what happens afterward. You'll also learn about the utensils and other equipment you'll want to have in place before you begin.

Selecting Your Bones

You can't produce a nourishing broth if you start with malnourished bones, so always be sure to buy the bones of humanely and organically raised animals. Use the following guidelines to help you source top-quality bones.

Stay Close to Nature

When an animal lives outside and is allowed to graze on its natural food, its bones retain higher levels of vitamins, minerals, healthy fats, and other nutrients than the bones of an animal raised in an industrial concentrated

animal feeding operation (CAFO)—and doesn't that phrase itself tell you everything you need to know about why the bones of grass-fed cattle are better for broth than the bones of cattle raised on soy, corn, and grain, not to mention the antibiotics needed to combat the CAFO's crowded, filthy conditions?

Choose Moving Bones and Marrowbones

When you want to use the bones of a large, humanely raised ruminant animal—a hoofed vegetarian that was allowed to roam through a pasture—pick bones that have moved a lot, since they'll have the highest collagen and gelatin content. The jointed bones of a ruminant animal are also ideal for broth. It's important to choose marrowbones, too, for what bone marrow contributes to the quality of your broth and its nutrients.

For Smaller Bones, Save Up or Splurge

All the bones of a smaller animal—a chicken, rabbit, or game bird, for example—can be used for broth. If you keep a resealable bag

TIPS FOR SOURCING BONES

Get to know a local farmer, or find a butcher who buys meat from a local farm. You'll be getting high-quality bones, and maybe your new friends will even give you a few scraps for being a good customer.

If you're buying meat and bones from a retail source, check the label. If the label doesn't say that the animal was organically raised and grass- or pasture-fed, then the animal likely wasn't raised or fed that way.

Pay attention to the size of the bones you are buying. You're probably not equipped to hack femur bones apart in your kitchen, so make sure the bones you purchase are a manageable size—small enough to fit in your chosen vessel and be completely covered with water.

The more exposed bone surfaces you have, the better for your broth. Whether you're buying directly from a farmer, getting your bones from a favorite butcher, or having bones shipped to you by a supplier, ask for knuckle bones to be quartered.

Choose crosscut bones. To make the most of the all-important bone marrow, use bones that have been cut horizontally into rounds 1 or 2 inches long so that the exposed marrow looks like a pink circle inside the lighter circle of bone. If you want to use longer bones, ask your supplier to expose the marrow by cutting the bones in half vertically.

Know your bones. Find out everything you can about where your bones are coming from and the conditions in which the animals were raised. Ask questions. Educate yourself. Good sources of information are the Animal Welfare Approved organization, the Farm-to-Consumer Legal Defense Fund, and the American Grassfed Association (see Resources, page 200).

in your freezer, you can save the bones from your preferred cuts until you accumulate enough to make a broth. Or you can simply put a whole carcass into your chosen cooking vessel at the end of a meal.

Go Nose to Tail

As modern consumers, we're used to buying meat in tidy little packages, which hide all signs that our food was once alive. But our grandmothers knew better. They understood that some of the most serious nourishment is concentrated in an animal's tendons, its neck, its knuckles, its feet, its tail, and even its head. So don't turn your back on the odd bits. Ask your supplier to include them in your order.

Basic Ingredients

Before I give you a shopping list, let's discuss two basic types of broth.

A *savory* broth is more traditional. It tends to be heavily seasoned with pungent vegetables, and it lends itself well to flavorful soups, stews, and meat-based dishes. This book includes many of my own original recipes for savory broths.

But this book is going to teach you how to cook outside the bone broth box, so we'll also be making *neutral* broths, which provide all the bone broth nutrients without the heavy seasoning. I came up with neutral bone broth one day when I discovered that I was out of all the usual vegetables and had to improvise. A neutral broth is great for people following the GAPS (gut and psychology syndrome) diet or the AIP (autoimmune protocol) diet. If you want, you can turn any savory broth recipe in this book into a recipe for a neutral broth (page 38).

And now for the shopping list! Once you have your bones, here are the basic ingredients you'll need for a savory broth:

- Onions
- Carrots
- Celery
- Fennel
- Apple cider vinegar
- Filtered water

And here are the basics for a neutral broth:

- Apple cider vinegar
- Filtered water
- Ginger, star anise, peppercorns (optional)

Needless to say, all these ingredients, just like your bones, should be organic and locally produced whenever possible.

First, You'll Need a Big Pot (aka the Equipment Section)

The big pot, of course, will be your primary cooking vessel as you make your bone broth at home. You have some options here; all will work well and have their own advantages, which we'll discuss in the cooking methods section to come. In addition to your cooking vessel of choice, you'll also need to get your hands on the following utensils and other items, which will come in handy for bone broth prep, cooking, and storage:

- Large, deep baking dish, lined with aluminum foil for easy cleanup
- Tongs
- Spider strainer
- Large fine-mesh strainer or, even better, a chinois
- Large vessel with a lid, into which the cooked broth will be strained
- Airtight containers for storing your broth

IS A PRESSURE COOKER RIGHT FOR YOU?

If you get serious about your romance with bone broth (your bro-mance?), consider buying a pressure cooker. It will reduce your cooking times by a factor of 30 to 50 percent. What's more, the shorter cooking times and the tightly sealed cooking pot mean that your broth will retain more nutrients while your house retains less of the aroma that comes with cooking bone broth. In addition, because the steam inside the cooking pot reaches such high temperatures, any harmful microorganisms are quickly killed, which also makes a pressure cooker ideal for sterilizing the mason jars used for canning and preserving foods. A pressure cooker saves energy, too.

It's true that the old-model stove top pressure cookers developed a reputation as the moody bad boys of the culinary world, prone to blowing their tops without warning. Your mother or your grandmother may have told you a tale about a pressure cooker gone wild. With practice, though, you can learn to read a stove top pressure cooker's warning signs.

But if you'd rather not flirt with danger, pick up one of the newer, electric models. If you follow the manufacturer's instructions, an electric pressure cooker is easy to use. Its safety features keep the lid on all that built-up pressure, and digital controls make your cooking experience virtually fail-safe. You can also use it to cook a variety of foods other than bone broth—everything from soup to cake.

You definitely have to be at home when you're using a stove top pressure cooker, and you should stick around while using an electric model, too. Play it safe—never leave any high-pressure appliance unattended while it's operating.

Here are some other optional items you might want to keep on hand:

- 1 or 2 chill sticks, which you can make yourself by filling stainless steel bottles with water and freezing them
- Cast iron or other metal pot for rendering the fat cap
- Grease screen for rendering the fat cap

Cooking Methods and Instructions

A big part of bone broth's appeal is the fact that you can cook it three different ways—on the stove top, in a slow cooker, or in a pressure cooker. Certain types of bones are better suited to certain types of vessels, but that doesn't mean you need a deluxe slow cooker or an expensive late-model pressure cooker before you can make a particular kind of broth. In reality, you can start very simply. Remember, my first slow cooker was a $3 model from the thrift store!

I don't recommend making bone broth in the oven. The minimum temperature of most standard ovens is 250°F, and bone broth needs to cook at a lower temperature. But if you can keep the temperature of your oven low enough (below 212°F), you can use it to cook bone broth in a large, deep dish—ovenproof, of course.

Since we're on the subject of cooking temperatures, I need to warn you that you never want your broth to come to a boil—if your broth begins to boil, the collagen and gelatin will break down. The boiling point for liquid is 212°F, so to protect the integrity of your broth, your cooking temperature always

has to be lower than that. But you also don't want the temperature to drop below 165°F. A simple simmer will bring your broth to the correct heat, but if you want to be precise, you can place a meat thermometer in the pot (don't let it touch the sides or the bottom). I've found that the best broth is produced with a cooking temperature between 190°F and 200°F.

Using the Stove Top

Using the stove top means being at home—no two ways about it. You can't safely leave the house when broth is simmering on an open flame. But I'm happy to be a stay-at-home chef when I'm preparing a short-cooking broth from the bones of fish, shellfish, poultry, or small game. Stove top cooking is actually the best method for bones like these. The risk of boiling your broth is primarily an issue when you're cooking it on the stove top, since you can put a slow cooker or a pressure cooker on a low setting. To make sure your broth doesn't boil, keep an eye on it. You'll start to be able to recognize the characteristically languid little dance that broth performs when it's at the perfect temperature. The liquid moves in a slow, lazy way, and small to medium bubbles come up from the bottom of the pot while pieces of meat and pools of liquefied fat float to the surface. (In a moment we'll talk about skimming the fat from cooked, cooled broth, but there's no need to skim liquid fat while your broth is cooking.)

Using a Slow Cooker

My personal preference when I'm making broth at home is to use my slow cooker. It can handle a variety of bones. Even better,

I can pretty much set it and forget it. Maybe I'll check in on it every now and then if I'm around—though I certainly won't want to raise the lid and dissipate all the lovely heat that's been building up! We have a cozy, low-maintenance relationship, my slow cooker and I. It's very undemanding of my time and attention. A 6-quart slow cooker will work best for the recipes in this book, though you can always adapt the recipes for a smaller model.

Using a Pressure Cooker

The pressure cooker is an aptly named device. Not only does it operate on the principle of contained steam pressure, it takes the pressure off a busy cook because it greatly reduces cooking times. There's a bit of a learning curve, but your investment in learning can produce big dividends in the form of convenience, time saved, and an even more nutritious broth.

Bone Broth Cooking Times

COOKING METHOD	COOKING TIME	GOOD FOR . . .
Stove top	12–48 hours	Fish, shellfish, poultry, small game
Slow cooker	12–48 hours	Poultry, small game, lamb, beef, pork
Pressure cooker	30 minutes–3 hours	Fish, shellfish, poultry, small game, lamb, beef, pork

Your Go-To Bone Broth Instructions

No matter what type of cooking vessel you use, the basic process of cooking bones for broth is the same. These step-by-step directions provide a great road map when making any kind of bone broth.

1. Preheat the oven to 425°F. I find that this temperature works well for roasting bones until they are very dark brown. Ovens vary, however, so you may find that you need to raise the temperature to 450°F to achieve that deep, dark color.

2. While the oven is preheating, rinse the bones, and rinse and chop the vegetables and/or aromatics. Line a deep baking dish with aluminum foil and grease the foil to prevent the bones from sticking.

3. If your bones are frozen, there's no need to thaw them. Simply put them in the foil-lined baking dish and brown them in the oven until they turn a very, very dark color (you don't want grayish broth). This will take 25 to 35 minutes.

4. Let the browned bones cool for about 10 minutes, and then transfer them to your chosen cooking vessel. Add the chopped vegetables and any other ingredients, and pour in enough water to cover completely.

5. Add the vinegar to the water, and let the mixture sit for 15 minutes so the minerals will be drawn out of the bones and into the broth.

6. Turn on the heat under your pot if you're cooking on the stove top, or put your slow cooker or pressure cooker on the desired

HOW TO STORE YOUR BROTH

Once you've finished cooking your bone broth, follow these guidelines to strain, cool, gel, skim, store, freeze, and thaw your broth.

Straining and cooling. Use a pair of long tongs to reach into the pot and remove the bones; you can discard them or reserve them for use in your next batch of broth (see page 32). Then use a spider strainer to lift out the vegetables and other solids, and discard them. At this point you can add one or two chill sticks to the broth to help cool it off more quickly. Let the broth cool at room temperature for 1 hour. Place a large fine-mesh strainer or chinois over a vessel large enough to hold the cooked broth, pour the broth through the strainer, and discard any bits of solid matter that the spider strainer missed. It's best to perform this straining operation over the sink.

Gelling. Cover the vessel and refrigerate for 24 hours.

Skimming. After 24 hours in the refrigerator, the broth should have a gelled consistency (broth gels naturally as it cools), and on top there should be a fairly thick layer of solidified fat (a fat cap). This fat has to be skimmed if you want to freeze the broth. To skim quickly and safely, use the blade of a butter knife to detach the fat cap gently from the side of the container, and then lift it out—if the broth has been properly cooled, the fat cap should pop right off. For broth that isn't going to be frozen, the fat can either be skimmed or left in place until the broth is used. Save this precious fat cap for rendering (see page 31).

Storing. You can store broth in airtight containers of any kind—mason jars, plastic tubs, or various sizes of resealable plastic bags; the particular type of container you choose will depend on the type and amount of your storage space. Broth will keep in the refrigerator for a week or two, but if you know you're not going to use it within a week of making it, freeze it instead.

Freezing. Broth will keep for up to 6 months in the freezer. But here's an important fact that I learned the hard way—liquid expands by about 9 percent when it's frozen. If you're planning to freeze your broth, you'll need to leave enough room at the top of your storage container for the broth to expand. Mason jars are cute, and they're great for the refrigerator, but the expansion factor means that some types of mason jars will crack in your freezer, and then you'll be forced to throw away your perfect batch of broth. So, be sure that any glass container you use comes with freezing guidelines on the jar. Plastic tubs are my first choice for freezing broth, followed by resealable plastic bags.

Thawing. Frozen broth can be left to thaw in the refrigerator for up to 3 days. You can speed up the thawing process by running hot water over the frozen container to loosen it from the broth. Once the broth has been removed, drop it into a pot and gently heat it to 165°F. You can drink the heated broth immediately, or you can store it in the refrigerator for later.

setting, and cook the bones for the appropriate time (your cooking time will depend on your cooking vessel as well as on the type of bones you're using).

Managing the Mess

Did I mention that when you make bone broth at home, you also make a mess? A big one? That's because bone broth contains large amounts of fats, and the fat gets everywhere. But I've developed a fast and easy cleanup method. Here's all you need:

- Paper towels, or a cloth towel dedicated to cleaning-up fat
- A sink full of hot water
- Distilled white vinegar
- A box of borax
- Liquid dish soap

And here's all you need to do:

1. Use paper towels or a towel for cleaning up fat to wipe off any cooking equipment or utensils that are heavily covered in liquid (hot) or solid (cold) fat. *Do not use your kitchen sponge for this task.*

2. Fill the sink with hot water.

3. Add 1 cup vinegar, ½ cup borax, and 4 or 5 squirts of dish soap to the hot water.

4. Let the greasy utensils and equipment soak in this mixture for at least 20 minutes. If you used a slow cooker or an electric pressure cooker, *do not soak the heating element. Instead, remove the interior crock or cooking pot and soak it in the hot, soapy water.*

5. After the utensils and equipment have been soaking in the sink for at least 20 minutes, remove any that are dishwasher-safe, rinse them under the faucet in very hot water, and put them in the dishwasher (if you have one, of course). If you're washing the items by hand, rinse them under the faucet in very hot water, wash them with a soapy sponge, and then clean the sponge by soaking it in a second mixture of hot water, vinegar, borax, and dish soap.

BONE BROTH ADD-INS

One of my favorite things about bone broth is that you can start with something neutral and then play with the flavors of every cup with simple add-ins. Just simmer the finished broth with a few aromatics and/or spices. Here are some of my go-to's:

- Orange and baking spices
- Fish sauce, lemon, and seaweed
- Sea salt and cracked pepper
- Lemon and raw honey
- Lemon and sea salt
- Cinnamon and raw cane sugar or raw honey
- Dried herbs
- Fresh sliced apple, raw honey, and cinnamon

FAQs

Why didn't my broth gel?

First of all, don't worry if your broth didn't gel. Mine didn't for the first eight months! Broth that hasn't gelled is still tasty, nutritious, and healing. In general, however, there are two reasons why broth doesn't gel: either a long cooking time breaks the collagen chains and keeps them from turning to gelatin, or the bones didn't contain enough collagen in the first place. If your broth didn't gel, try reducing the cooking time, or give your broth a gelatin boost by tossing some feet and tendons into the mix. Note also that non-gelled bone broth is my first choice for cold beverages, since I don't care for a gelatinous texture when I'm drinking. So, if you do end up with non-gelled broth, consider it a good opportunity to try one of the recipes in chapter 4!

How will cooking broth for hours or days affect the way my house smells?

Cooking broth for hours or days will make your house smell like broth, and the aroma will stick around for a little while. But it's just part of the experience, and you'll find yourself getting used to it. You'll probably even come to enjoy it.

What should I do with all the fat?

You can render it for use as a cooking fat. Rich in nutritional value, with a high smoke point and a delicious taste, this is one of the healthiest fats you can cook with. Don't discard this kitchen treasure! Instead, follow these instructions: Skim the fat cap from your cooked and cooled broth, put it in a deep cast-iron or other metal pot, and set the pot over low heat (you don't want the fat to burn). Cover the pot with a grease screen topped by two paper towels and simmer the fat until all the bubbles have disappeared and you no longer hear any popping or crackling coming from the pot, 15 to 30 minutes. (These noisy little bubbles are the liquid evaporating from the fat.) Once the fat has been completely rendered, it should look smooth and lucid and make no noise. It's now ready for use in cooking, or you can store it for later.

And here's another simple opportunity for adding to your store of rendered fat for cooking: The liquid that collects in the baking dish when bones are browned is fat that has rendered itself. Pour this rendered fat through a fine-mesh strainer right into your mason jar.

Rendered fat can be stored in the refrigerator or at room temperature (because it was not cooked in liquid, or you have removed the liquid through the rendering process, it is shelf-stable). Fat that was properly rendered will last almost indefinitely. Always make sure that the fat has a slight beefy aroma before you use it—the smell should never be strong or rancid.

How can I tell if my bone broth has gone bad?

There's no mistaking the putrid smell of broth gone bad. You couldn't make yourself consume it even if you wanted to. But bone broth doesn't have to smell flat-out disgusting before it's a candidate for the garbage. If your broth smells even the slightest bit off, throw it out immediately.

What if I don't like the taste of the broth I made?

Next time try adding some apple cider vinegar, ginger, salt, or other spices and aromatics either in the cooking process or right before you're ready to consume it. Sometimes the tiniest change makes the biggest difference. Or consider making a neutral broth instead of a savory one (see page 38).

What should I do with the leftover bones?

Cook them again! I don't recommend using them more than three times, but you can get a perfectly good broth by mixing used bones with new ones. Or you can recook the used bones by themselves to produce second- or third-run bone broth. I like adding this recycled broth to pet food, but don't add the bones themselves—in June 2015 the US Food and

BONE BROTH FOR ANY SEASON

Winter
Add your favorite warming spices, such as cinnamon or nutmeg, to hot bone broth.

Spring
Perk up your broth with citrus, vinegars, or fermented juices.

Summer
Whip up a batch of "brothtails"— add second- or third-run (non-gelled) bone broth to iced drinks.

Fall
Move over, latte— time for a pumpkin-spiced bone broth.

By now you must be tempted. You'd like to get acquainted with bone broth. You're even thinking you might become serious about bone broth. But what if your affair with bone broth turns out to be nothing more than a winter fling?

Not a chance!

As you may recall, I have dental implants from a childhood skiing accident. My implants depend on healthy bones, so I drink bone broth all year long. That's just one reason why I've become so creative about varying my recipes with the changing of the seasons.

Here are my secrets for keeping the flame alive after winter nights give way to spring mornings, long summer days, and crisp autumn afternoons.

Drug Administration issued a warning against giving bones to pets, so feel free to share your broth with Fido, but keep raw and cooked bones where he can't get at them.

About the Recipes

The recipes in this book are designed to make bone broth and all of its wellness benefits a frequent addition to your daily meals. You'll find simple recipes for basic broths, as well as some that are a little more out-of-the-box. Healing tonics and rejuvenating drinks offer a quick way to enjoy more bone broth, but I've also included plenty of ideas for broth-based dishes to make bone broth an integral part of every meal of the day—breakfast, lunch, dinner, and yes, even desserts. One of the many beautiful things about bone broth is that it does not lose any of its healing properties when it is cooked—it just becomes denser.

We don't all follow the same diet, so I've included recipe labels throughout the book to indicate whether a recipe is dairy-free, gluten-free, or Paleo. Since all of our eating habits are different, some recipes include multiple options for an ingredient. For example, for cooking fats you will be provided with your choice of butter, ghee, tallow, or lard. Butter and ghee are not dairy-free, but tallow and lard are. Use the option that works for you. In this case, the recipe will be labeled dairy-free because it gives a dairy-free option, even though the other option contains dairy.

Another recipe label you'll find in this book is for a cook time under 30 minutes. We all know that making bone broth takes time. The good news is that once you have a batch, it can go a long way. Several recipes for cooking with bone broth are designed with busy weekdays in mind and can be completed in 30 minutes or less.

Getting the Most Out of Your Broth

One of the best things about bone broth is that your body doesn't care how you consume it. Bone broth's nutrients don't disappear when you cook, freeze, store, or thaw the broth. You can heat your broth and sip it from a mug, add it cold to an iced drink, use it as a soup base, or whisk it into a sauce. Whatever your approach, your body gets all the benefits.

And what's really cool—and maybe even a little bit spooky—is that bone broth actually seems to *know* which parts of your body are most in need of its healing effects. Remember what I said earlier about the positive changes in my skin, and the disappearance of my chronic bone pain, and the soothing of my stomach after I'd been drinking bone broth for less than a year? I didn't start drinking bone broth with the idea of resolving any health issues—I just thought it sounded good, and I wanted to try it. And I didn't tell the broth's nutrients where to go or what to do— they just went to where they were needed and brought about changes that were healing for me. In fact, it's because of stories like mine that practitioners of Eastern medicine talk about bone broth as an "intelligent" food.

So why not be smart and raise bone broth's IQ even higher? As we discussed in chapter 1, you can do that by making bone broth a lifestyle choice—by incorporating it into a diet based on authentic, whole, traditional foods; a diet that includes humanely produced meats, lots of sustainably farmed organic local produce, and a variety of probiotics and fermented items.

I hope the rest of this offers you a steady stream of fresh insights. I'll be giving you clear instructions for making and using different types of bone broth, with lots of variations, but you're free to be as creative as you like. Play around with what piques your interest and your taste buds, and move on from—or, better yet, improve on—anything that doesn't.

I want you to think of this book as a reference, a reliable source you can turn to again and again when you have questions or just need a shot of culinary inspiration. I hope you'll read it not just once but many times. Keep coming back. Use the recipes every day, and integrate the book into your life. Let it become your trusted companion on your journey toward better health and greater, more radiant wellness.

CHAPTER 3

BASIC BROTHS AND TONICS

Making your own bone broth doesn't need to be complicated or terribly time consuming. Most of the recipes included here are, in fact, very simple. In this chapter you'll find ten essential broth recipes, ranging from your basic beef and chicken to the more adventurous rabbit and wild game.

I've followed these basics with ten recipes for broth tonics designed to give your broth targeted wellness benefits. Some are simple, some are more complex, but all will have you singing the song of optimal health. And don't forget to be creative when making your broth; if you don't happen to like the taste of a particular ingredient, you don't have to use it. That's the beauty of making your own; you can tailor your creations to your preferences.

You can also make a secondary bone broth batch from the same set of bones. Technically speaking, you can make continuous batches of broth from the same bones until the bones completely dissolve. Of course, the more batches of bone broth you produce using the same bones, the less potent the broth will be. I have never gotten to the completely dissolved point, but I did once make 12 batches from the same bones as an experiment. Each batch became weaker and weaker. Consequently, I don't suggest running bones through more than three batches. You can, however, use bones that have been through one to three batches along with new bones and create a great bone broth. This will help you save on your household budget. Personally, I like to use my second and third batches of bone broth for cold drinks (see chapter 4).

MAKING NEUTRAL BONE BROTH

Some of the recipes in this book call for using a neutral bone broth. This is most common in beverages and other recipes where the flavor of onions, garlic, and other vegetables is less desirable. To make a neutral bone broth, follow any of the bone broth recipes in this chapter, but omit the vegetables. Instead, substitute 2 (3-inch) pieces of ginger, thinly sliced, and, if desired, a small bulb of sliced fennel. Cook the bone broth according to the recipe directions, and label it for use in recipes calling for neutral broth.

General Tips to Keep in Mind Before You Get Started

IF YOU'RE NEW TO BONE BROTH, remember you will be on a learning curve for the first few runs as you figure out what methods work best for you.

MAKE SURE YOU GREASE THE ALUMINUM FOIL WHEN ROASTING THE BONES. This will make them easy to remove from the baking dish (they tend to get stuck), and will also make for easier cleanup and fat saving.

BE SURE YOU DON'T LET YOUR BONE BROTH BOIL. Boiling breaks down that good collagen and gelatin. I've found that the best broth is produced with a cooking temperature between 190°F and 200°F.

FOLLOW THE FAT-SAVING TIPS on page 31 for baking-dish fat and rendered fat, and discover the benefits of natural fat.

IF YOU ARE USING A PRESSURE COOKER, I recommend that you add chill sticks (see page 27) to the cooling broth. Because of the very high temperature at which it was cooked, it takes additional time to cool down and can heat up your refrigerator.

Beef Bone Broth

Makes 4 to 6 quarts

PREP
30 minutes,
plus 1 day to cool

COOK
20 minutes, plus

Slow Cooker:
24 to 36 hours

Stove Top:
24 to 36 hours

Pressure Cooker:
2 hours

This classic bone broth uses knuckle and marrowbones; their collagen and fat yield a rich-textured and nourishing liquid. The carrot, onion, and fennel all add a hint of sweetness, while celery and garlic help balance the flavors and add depth. Adding more vegetables or bones will create a more complex flavor.

3 pounds mixed beef knuckle and marrowbones
1 tablespoon apple cider vinegar
2 celery stalks, chopped
1 carrot, chopped
½ white onion, sliced
½ medium fennel bulb, cored and sliced
1 garlic clove, cut in half

1. Preheat the oven to 425°F.

2. Put the frozen or thawed knuckle and marrowbones in a deep baking dish lined with greased aluminum foil. Roast the bones until they are a deep, dark brown color, about 30 minutes. Remove from the oven and let cool for 10 minutes.

3. Transfer the bones to a large slow cooker, stockpot, or pressure cooker. Fill the vessel with filtered water, enough to completely cover the bones, and add the apple cider vinegar. Allow the bones to sit in the water and vinegar for 15 minutes. Add all the remaining ingredients to the vessel, and follow one of these cooking methods:

   SLOW COOKER: Turn the slow cooker to the low setting and cook for 24 to 36 hours.

   STOVE TOP: Bring the broth to a low simmer over medium heat, making sure to never reach the point of boiling. Aim for a slow movement in the broth, with small to medium bubbles rising from the bottom. Cook for 24 to 36 hours.

   PRESSURE COOKER: Bring the pressure cooker to high heat, and then lower the heat once it has reached between 10 and 15 psi. Cook for 2 hours. Always follow the manufacturer's directions, and never leave a pressure cooker unattended. ▶

Beef Bone Broth continued

4. When the broth is done, it will be a rich, dark brown color. Use tongs to carefully remove the bones from the broth, and discard (or reserve to use again). Use a spider strainer to remove the vegetables, and discard. Let the broth cool for 1 hour.

5. Set a large fine-mesh strainer over a storage container. Carefully pour the cooled broth into the container. Cover the container and transfer it to the refrigerator for 24 hours.

6. Remove the lid, discard the fat layer from the stock or reserve for rendering (see page 31), and use as desired.

Chicken Bone Broth

Makes 4 to 6 quarts

PREP
20 minutes,
plus 1 day to cool

COOK
20 minutes, plus

Slow Cooker:
8 to 12 hours

Stove Top:
8 to 12 hours

Pressure Cooker:
30 to 45 minutes

While this broth is reminiscent of good old-fashioned chicken soup, it is much lighter and milder. The more bones you use, the more intense your final broth will be. Because most of the fat lies in and just beneath the skin, this broth is relatively low-fat. The fennel adds some sweetness and a licorice-like note.

1 chicken carcass
2 tablespoons apple cider vinegar
2 celery stalks, chopped
1 carrot, chopped
½ white onion, sliced
½ medium fennel bulb, cored and sliced
1 garlic clove, cut in half

1. Preheat the oven to 425°F.

2. Put the frozen or thawed chicken bones in a deep baking dish lined with greased aluminum foil. Roast the bones until they are a deep, dark brown color, about 20 minutes. Remove from the oven and let cool for 10 minutes.

3. Transfer the bones to a large slow cooker, stockpot, or pressure cooker. Fill the vessel with filtered water, enough to completely cover the bones, and add the apple cider vinegar. Allow the bones to sit in the water and vinegar for 15 minutes. Add all the remaining ingredients to the vessel and follow one of these cooking methods:

SLOW COOKER: Turn the slow cooker to the low setting and cook for 8 to 12 hours.

STOVE TOP: Bring the broth to a low simmer over medium heat, making sure to never reach the point of boiling. Aim for a slow movement in the broth, with small to medium bubbles rising from the bottom. Cook for 8 to 12 hours.

PRESSURE COOKER: Bring the pressure cooker to high heat, and then lower the heat once it has reached between 10 and 15 psi. Cook for 30 to 45 minutes. Always follow the manufacturer's directions, and never leave a pressure cooker unattended. ▶

Chicken Bone Broth continued

4. When the broth is done, it will be a deep golden color. Use tongs to carefully remove the bones from the broth, and discard (or reserve to use again). Use a spider strainer to remove the vegetables, and discard. Let the broth cool for 1 hour.

5. Set a large fine-mesh strainer over a storage container. Carefully pour the cooled broth into the container. Cover the container and transfer it to the refrigerator for 24 hours.

6. Remove the lid, discard the fat layer from the stock or reserve for rendering (see page 31), and use as desired.

Duck Bone Broth

Makes 4 to 6 quarts

PREP
20 minutes,
plus 1 day to cool

COOK
20 minutes, plus

Slow Cooker:
8 to 12 hours

Stove Top:
8 to 12 hours

Pressure Cooker:
30 to 45 minutes

Duck meat is rich and full of flavor; not surprisingly, duck bones are the base of a standard French stock. Look for duck necks if possible—they are typically inexpensive but will yield a very satisfying broth. Shallots and leeks are classic ingredients used in duck stock, so you may want to consider them as well as you customize this recipe to your liking.

1 duck carcass
2 tablespoons apple cider vinegar
2 celery stalks, chopped
1 carrot, chopped
½ white onion, sliced
½ medium fennel bulb, cored and sliced
1 garlic clove, cut in half

1. Preheat the oven to 425°F.

2. Put the frozen or thawed duck bones in a deep baking dish lined with greased aluminum foil. Roast the bones until they are a deep, dark brown color, about 20 minutes. Remove from the oven and let cool for 10 minutes.

3. Transfer the bones to a large slow cooker, stockpot, or pressure cooker. Fill the vessel with filtered water, enough to completely cover the bones, and add the apple cider vinegar. Allow the bones to sit in the water and vinegar for 15 minutes. Add all the remaining ingredients to the vessel, and follow one of these cooking methods:

SLOW COOKER: Turn the slow cooker to the low setting and cook for 8 to 12 hours.

STOVE TOP: Bring the broth to a low simmer over medium heat, making sure to never reach the point of boiling. Aim for a slow movement in the broth, with small to medium bubbles rising from the bottom. Cook for 8 to 12 hours.

PRESSURE COOKER: Bring the pressure cooker to high heat, and then lower the heat once it has reached between 10 and 15 psi. Cook for 30 to 45 minutes. Always follow the manufacturer's directions, and never leave a pressure cooker unattended.

4. When the broth is done, it will be a rich mahogany color. Use tongs to carefully remove the bones from the broth, and discard (or reserve to use again). Use a spider strainer to remove the vegetables, and discard. Let the broth cool for 1 hour.

5. Set a large fine-mesh strainer over a storage container. Carefully pour the cooled broth into the container. Cover the container and transfer it to the refrigerator for 24 hours.

6. Remove the lid, discard the fat layer from the stock or reserve for rendering (see page 31), and use as desired.

Lamb Bone Broth

Makes 4 to 6 quarts

PREP
20 minutes,
plus 1 day to cool

COOK
20 minutes, plus

Slow Cooker:
24 to 36 hours

Stove Top:
24 to 36 hours

Pressure Cooker:
1 to 2 hours

Lamb is often included in elimination diets because it is easy for most people to tolerate. If you have allergies or food issues, you may find lamb bone broth the most soothing, therefore it's a good broth for beginning your journey. Use the basic formula here; if you want to prepare it more in the style of stock, add celery leaves, parsley stems, a clove, and peppercorns.

3 pounds mixed lamb bones
2 tablespoons apple cider vinegar
2 celery stalks, chopped
1 carrot, chopped
½ white onion, sliced
½ medium fennel bulb, cored and sliced
1 garlic clove, cut in half

1. Preheat the oven to 425°F.

2. Put the frozen or thawed lamb bones in a deep baking dish lined with greased aluminum foil. Roast the bones until they are a deep, dark brown color, about 20 minutes. Remove from the oven and let cool for 10 minutes.

3. Transfer the bones to a large slow cooker, stockpot, or pressure cooker. Fill the vessel with filtered water, enough to completely cover the bones, and add the apple cider vinegar. Allow the bones to sit in the water and vinegar for 15 minutes. Add all the remaining ingredients to the vessel, and follow one of these cooking methods:

SLOW COOKER: Turn the slow cooker to the low setting and cook for 24 to 36 hours.

STOVE TOP: Bring the broth to a low simmer over medium heat, making sure to never reach the point of boiling. Aim for a slow movement in the broth, with small to medium bubbles rising from the bottom. Cook for 24 to 36 hours.

PRESSURE COOKER: Bring the pressure cooker to high heat, and then lower the heat once it has reached between 10 and 15 psi. Cook for 1 to 2 hours. Always follow the manufacturer's directions, and never leave a pressure cooker unattended.

4. When the broth is done, it will be a rich, dark brown color. Use tongs to carefully remove the bones from the broth and discard (or reserve to use again). Use a spider strainer to remove the vegetables, and discard. Let the broth cool for 1 hour.

5. Set a large fine-mesh strainer over a storage container. Carefully pour the cooled broth into the container. Cover the container and transfer it to the refrigerator for 24 hours.

6. Remove the lid, discard the fat layer from the stock or reserve for rendering (see page 31), and use as desired.

Pork Bone Broth

Makes 4 to 6 quarts

PREP
20 minutes,
plus 1 day to cool

COOK
20 minutes, plus

Slow Cooker:
24 to 36 hours

Stove Top:
24 to 36 hours

Pressure Cooker:
1 to 2 hours

While pork bones are not traditionally used for stock, they are a perfectly good choice since they are flavorful and rich in collagen. A variety of different bones will yield excellent flavor and texture, and using the best-quality pasture-raised pork bones will give you a delightfully tasty broth that is less expensive than beef or chicken. Be sure to remove the fat from this broth for a cleaner flavor.

3 pounds pork bones (knuckles, shanks, leg bones)
2 tablespoons apple cider vinegar
2 celery stalks, chopped
1 carrot, chopped
½ white onion, sliced
½ medium fennel bulb, cored and sliced
1 garlic clove, cut in half

1. Preheat the oven to 425°F.

2. Put the frozen or thawed pork bones in a deep baking dish lined with greased aluminum foil. Roast the bones until they are a deep, dark brown color, about 20 minutes. Remove from the oven and let cool for 10 minutes.

3. Transfer the bones to a large slow cooker, stockpot, or pressure cooker. Fill the vessel with filtered water, enough to completely cover the bones, and add the apple cider vinegar. Allow the bones to sit in the water and vinegar for 15 minutes. Add all the remaining ingredients to the vessel, and follow one of these cooking methods:

SLOW COOKER: Turn the slow cooker to the low setting and cook for 24 to 36 hours.

STOVE TOP: Bring the broth to a low simmer over medium heat, making sure to never reach the point of boiling. Aim for a slow movement in the broth, with small to medium bubbles rising from the bottom. Cook for 24 to 36 hours.

PRESSURE COOKER: Bring the pressure cooker to high heat, and then lower the heat once it has reached between 10 and 15 psi. Cook for 1 to 2 hours. Always follow the manufacturer's directions, and never leave a pressure cooker unattended.

4. When the broth is done, it will be a rich, dark brown color. Use tongs to carefully remove the bones from the broth, and discard (or reserve to use again). Use a spider strainer to remove the vegetables, and discard. Let the broth cool for 1 hour.

5. Set a large fine-mesh strainer over a storage container. Carefully pour the cooled broth into the container. Cover the container and transfer it to the refrigerator for 24 hours.

6. Remove the lid, discard the fat layer from the stock or reserve for rendering (see page 31), and use as desired.

Mixed Bone Broth

Makes 4 to 6 quarts

PREP
20 minutes,
plus 1 day to cool

COOK
20 minutes, plus

Slow Cooker:
24 to 36 hours

Stove Top:
24 to 36 hours

Pressure Cooker:
1 to 2 hours

When you don't have a large enough quantity of any particular bone, a mixed bone broth is an easy way to combine and use what you have on hand to make something nourishing. The flavor will vary depending upon the types of bones you use. Meat bones typically have a stronger flavor than poultry, so you may want to combine either all meat or all poultry bones to create a more harmonious and balanced broth.

3 pounds mixed pork, chicken, or beef bones
2 tablespoons apple cider vinegar
2 celery stalks, chopped
1 carrot, chopped
½ white onion, sliced
½ medium fennel bulb, cored and sliced
1 garlic clove, cut in half

1. Preheat the oven to 425°F.

2. Put the frozen or thawed pork, chicken, or beef bones in a deep baking dish lined with greased aluminum foil. Roast the bones until they are a deep, dark brown color, about 20 minutes. Remove from the oven and let cool for 10 minutes.

3. Transfer the bones to a large slow cooker, stockpot, or pressure cooker. Fill the vessel with filtered water, enough to completely cover the bones, and add the apple cider vinegar. Allow the bones to sit in the water and vinegar for 15 minutes. Add all the remaining ingredients to the vessel, and follow one of these cooking methods:

SLOW COOKER: Turn the slow cooker to the low setting and cook for 24 to 36 hours.

STOVE TOP: Bring the broth to a low simmer over medium heat, making sure to never reach the point of boiling. Aim for a slow movement in the broth, with small to medium bubbles rising from the bottom. Cook for 24 to 36 hours.

PRESSURE COOKER: Bring the pressure cooker to high heat, and then lower the heat once it has reached between 10 and 15 psi. Cook for 1 to 2 hours. Always follow the manufacturer's directions, and never leave a pressure cooker unattended.

4. When the broth is done it will be a rich, dark brown color. Use tongs to carefully remove the bones from the broth, and discard (or reserve to use again). Use a spider strainer to remove the vegetables, and discard. Let the broth cool for 1 hour.

5. Set a large fine-mesh strainer over a storage container. Carefully pour the cooled broth into the container. Cover the container and transfer it to the refrigerator for 24 hours.

6. Remove the lid, discard the fat layer from the stock or reserve for rendering (see page 31), and use as desired.

THE BROTHS

Rabbit Bone Broth

Makes 4 to 6 quarts

PREP
20 minutes,
plus 1 day to cool

COOK
20 minutes, plus

Slow Cooker:
24 hours

Stove Top:
24 hours

Pressure Cooker:
1 to 1½ hours

Rabbit is one of the most sustainable of all meats, and the broth from its bones is silky and full-bodied. The flavor is relatively mild and may remind you of chicken broth. Rabbit broth makes a good basic broth to be used in other recipes and tonics. If you want to add an herbal component, try bay leaves or parsley.

1 rabbit carcass
¼ cup apple cider vinegar
2 celery stalks, chopped
1 carrot, chopped
½ white onion, sliced
½ medium fennel bulb, cored and sliced
1 garlic clove, cut in half

1. Preheat the oven to 425°F.

2. Put the frozen or thawed rabbit bones in a deep baking dish lined with greased aluminum foil. Roast the bones until they are a deep, dark brown color, about 20 minutes. Remove from the oven and let cool for 10 minutes.

3. Transfer the bones to a large slow cooker, stockpot, or pressure cooker. Fill the vessel with filtered water, enough to completely cover the bones, and add the apple cider vinegar. Allow the bones to sit in the water and vinegar for 15 minutes. Add all the remaining ingredients to the vessel, and follow one of these cooking methods:

SLOW COOKER: Turn the slow cooker to the low setting and cook for 24 hours.

STOVE TOP: Bring the broth to a low simmer over medium heat, making sure to never reach the point of boiling. Aim for a slow movement in the broth, with small to medium bubbles rising from the bottom. Cook for 24 hours.

PRESSURE COOKER: Bring the pressure cooker to high heat, and then lower the heat once it has reached between 10 and 15 psi. Cook for 1 to 1½ hours. Always follow the manufacturer's directions, and never leave a pressure cooker unattended.

4. When the broth is done, it will be a rich, dark brown color. Use tongs to carefully remove the bones from the broth, and discard (or reserve to use again). Use a spider strainer to remove the vegetables, and discard. Let the broth cool for 1 hour.

5. Set a large fine-mesh strainer over a storage container. Carefully pour the cooled broth into the container. Cover the container and transfer it to the refrigerator for 24 hours.

6. Remove the lid, discard the fat layer from the stock or reserve for rendering (see page 31), and use as desired.

Wild Game Bone Broth

Makes 4 to 6 quarts

PREP
20 minutes,
plus 1 day to cool

COOK
20 minutes, plus

Slow Cooker:
24 to 36 hours

Stove Top:
24 to 36 hours

Pressure Cooker:
1 to 2 hours

► To prevent gamy broth: The night before you plan to prepare the broth, put the bones in a large bowl and add enough milk to cover. Cover the bowl and transfer to the refrigerator. Allow the bones to soak for 12 to 24 hours to neutralize some of the gaminess. Drain and rinse the bones.

Wild game consists of any meat that is hunted rather than raised on a farm; it can be higher in protein, lower in fat, and higher in healthy fats. It's also free from added synthetic hormones and antibiotics. Meat from wild game can sometimes taste gamy depending on the season the animal was harvested and what it was eating at the time, but since you are just using the bones here, this is less likely to be an issue. (See the Tip if your broth turns out excessively gamy.)

3 pounds wild game bones (such as venison, wild boar, antelope, or game birds)
6 tablespoons apple cider vinegar
2 celery stalks, chopped
1 carrot, chopped
½ white onion, sliced
½ medium fennel bulb, cored and sliced
1 garlic clove, cut in half

1. Preheat the oven to 425°F.

2. Put the bones in a deep baking dish lined with greased aluminum foil. Roast the bones until they are a deep, dark brown color, about 20 minutes. Remove from the oven and let cool for 10 minutes.

3. Transfer the bones to a large slow cooker, stockpot, or pressure cooker. Fill the vessel with filtered water, enough to completely cover the bones, and add the apple cider vinegar. Allow the bones to sit in the water and vinegar for 15 minutes. Add all the remaining ingredients to the vessel, and follow one of these cooking methods:

SLOW COOKER: Turn the slow cooker to the low setting and cook for 24 to 36 hours.

STOVE TOP: Bring the broth to a low simmer over medium heat, making sure to never reach the point of boiling. Aim for a slow movement in the broth, with small to medium bubbles rising from the bottom. Cook for 24 to 36 hours.

PRESSURE COOKER: Bring the pressure cooker to high heat, and then lower the heat once it has reached between 10 and 15 psi. Cook for 1 to 2 hours. Always follow the manufacturer's directions, and never leave a pressure cooker unattended.

4. When the broth is done, it will be a rich, dark brown color. Use tongs to carefully remove the bones from the broth, and discard (or reserve to use again). Use a spider strainer to remove the vegetables, and discard. Leave the broth to cool for 1 hour.

5. Set a large fine-mesh strainer over a storage container. Carefully pour the cooled broth into the container. Cover the container and transfer it to the refrigerator for 24 hours.

6. Remove the lid, discard the fat layer from the stock or reserve for rendering (see page 31), and use as desired.

Fish Bone Broth

Makes 4 to 6 quarts

PREP
20 minutes,
plus 1 day to cool

COOK
10 minutes, plus

Slow Cooker:
4 to 6 hours

Stove Top:
4 to 6 hours

Pressure Cooker:
20 to 30 minutes

▶ The bones of white fish, such as sole, flounder, snapper, and bass, are preferable and will create a light and delicate broth. On the other hand, oily fish such as salmon and mackerel will yield a strong flavor and greasy texture that may be less palatable.

Fish stock, made from bones and vegetables, is a classic ingredient used in soups, chowders, and sauces. Nutritious fish bone broth can be prepared using any mild non-oily fish.

2 fish heads
1 pound fish bones
¼ cup apple cider vinegar
2 celery stalks, chopped
1 carrot, chopped
½ white onion, sliced
½ medium fennel bulb, cored and sliced
1 garlic clove, cut in half

1. Preheat the oven to 375°F.

2. Put the fish heads and bones in a deep baking dish lined with greased aluminum foil. Roast the bones for 10 minutes to release their oils.

3. Transfer the bones to a slow cooker, stockpot, or pressure cooker. Fill the vessel with filtered water, enough to completely cover the bones, and add the apple cider vinegar. Allow the bones to sit in the water and vinegar for 15 minutes. Skim off any scum that forms on the surface. Add all the remaining ingredients to the vessel, and follow one of these cooking methods:

SLOW COOKER: Turn the slow cooker to the low setting and cook for 4 to 6 hours. Several times during the cooking, skim off any scum that forms on the surface, and discard.

STOVE TOP: Bring the broth to a low simmer over medium heat, making sure to never reach the point of boiling. Aim for a slow movement in the broth, with small to medium bubbles rising from the bottom. Cook for 4 to 6 hours. Several times during the cooking, skim off any scum that forms on the surface, and discard.

PRESSURE COOKER: Bring the pressure cooker to high heat, and then lower the heat once it has reached between 10 and 15 psi. Cook for 20 to 30 minutes. Always follow the manufacturer's directions, and never leave a pressure cooker unattended.

4. When the broth is done, it will be a pale golden color. If you used a slow cooker or stove top stockpot, use a spider strainer to remove the fish bones and vegetables, and discard. If you used a pressure cooker, strain the broth through a cheesecloth-lined colander into a large bowl. Press the bones and vegetables against the sides of the colander with a spoon to extract even more flavor. Let the broth cool for 1 hour.

5. Set a large fine-mesh strainer over a storage container. Carefully pour the cooled broth into the container. Cover the container and transfer it to the refrigerator for 24 hours.

6. Remove the lid, discard the fat layer (if any), and use the stock as desired.

Shellfish Broth

Makes 2 to 3 quarts

PREP
20 minutes,
plus 1 day to cool

COOK
10 minutes, plus

Slow Cooker:
2 to 4 hours

Stove Top:
2 to 4 hours

Pressure Cooker:
20 to 30 minutes

Any shellfish shells and heads will yield a surprisingly rich and colorful broth. Traditionally used in many recipes, this broth has a very strong flavor. Because it is made from only the shells, it is very low in fat. Herbs such as thyme and bay will complement the broth; other options include tarragon and parsley, using either the stems or leaves or both.

4 to 6 cups broken-up crab, lobster, and/or shrimp shells
2 tablespoons apple cider vinegar
½ white onion, sliced
1 carrot, thinly sliced
½ medium fennel bulb, cored and sliced
1 garlic clove, cut in half
2 celery stalks, chopped
1 fresh thyme sprig
1 bay leaf
15 to 20 peppercorns

1. Preheat the oven to 400°F.

2. Put the shells in a deep baking dish lined with greased aluminum foil. Roast the shells for 10 minutes to release the oils and flavors. Transfer the shells to a large slow cooker, stockpot, or pressure cooker.

3. Fill the vessel with filtered water, enough to completely cover the shells, and add the apple cider vinegar. Allow the shells to sit in the water and vinegar for 15 minutes. Add all the remaining ingredients to the vessel, and follow one of these cooking methods:

SLOW COOKER: Turn the slow cooker to the low setting and cook for 2 to 4 hours. Several times during the cooking, skim off any scum that forms on the surface, and discard.

STOVE TOP: Bring the broth to a low simmer over medium heat, making sure to never reach the point of boiling. Aim for a slow movement in the broth, with small to medium bubbles rising from the bottom. Simmer for 2 to 4 hours. Several times during the cooking, skim off any scum that forms on the surface, and discard.

PRESSURE COOKER: Bring the pressure cooker to high heat, and then lower the heat once it has reached between 10 and 15 psi. Cook for 20 to 30 minutes. Always follow the manufacturer's directions, and never leave a pressure cooker unattended.

4. When the broth is done, it will be a golden and/or slightly pinkish color. If you used a slow cooker or stove top stockpot, use a spider strainer to remove the shells and vegetables, and discard. If you used a pressure cooker, strain the broth through a cheesecloth-lined colander into a large bowl. Press the shells and vegetables against the sides of the colander with a spoon to extract even more flavor. Let the broth cool for 1 hour.

5. Set a large fine-mesh strainer over a storage container or jar. Carefully pour the cooled broth into the container. Cover the container and transfer it to the refrigerator for 24 hours.

6. Remove the lid, discard the fat layer (if any), and use the stock as desired.

Joint Soother

Serves 1

PREP
5 minutes

COOK
5 minutes (plus
10 to 15 minutes
steeping time)

▶ For added relief,
take a cod liver oil
supplement with this
regimen.

Healthy fats in bone broth can help supply the necessary lubrication for a joint-healthy diet. I designed this tonic to help alleviate joint pain by adding natural anti-inflammatory ingredients to the broth: cayenne, a cousin to ginger, has long been known for its pain-relieving properties, while turmeric is classified as a curcuminoid; beneficial when it comes to inflammation. Finally, the addition of fermented juice to this tonic aids your gut with probiotics.

1¾ cups bone broth of your choice (Chapter 3)
1 tablespoon minced fresh ginger or 1 teaspoon ground ginger
1 teaspoon cayenne pepper
1½ teaspoons ground turmeric
1 tablespoon sauerkraut juice

1. In a small saucepan, heat the broth to a simmer.

2. In a large mug, combine the remaining ingredients. Pour the hot broth into the mug, cover, and steep for 10 to 15 minutes. Serve.

Pregnancy Broth

Serves 1

PREP
5 minutes

COOK
5 minutes (plus 10 to 15 minutes steeping time)

▶ Not only does apple cider vinegar add a little additional flavor to your drink, it can also help regulate your blood sugar. Add a generous splash to this beverage to increase its value to your body.

This tonic made from a combination of bone broth and herbal teas is designed to soothe nausea, increase iron levels, and improve your immune system. You can make your own tea by measuring and combining dried herbs, or add a tea bag of each of the dried herbs individually. You'll find both nettle and echinacea teas available in most natural health stores. Most important, remember to always check with your doctor before taking herbs during pregnancy.

1¾ cups neutral bone broth of your choice (page 38)
1 tablespoon minced fresh ginger
1 tablespoon dried echinacea
1 tablespoon nettles or 1 nettle teabag
2 fresh peppermint sprigs or 1½ teaspoons dried peppermint

1. In a small saucepan, heat the broth to a simmer.

2. Turn off the heat and add the remaining ingredients to the pan. Steep for 10 to 15 minutes.

3. Pour the tea through a strainer, discard the herbs, and serve.

Cleansing Broth

Serves 1

PREP
5 minutes

COOK
5 minutes

▶ If you choose to do a cleanse, always listen to your body! If you feel that you need to eat, please do.

This is one of my favorite ways to drink bone broth. A great morning pick-me-up, this broth gets your body going in all the right ways. The combination of lemon juice, apple cider vinegar, cayenne pepper, and molasses is an excellent way to cleanse and detox the body.

1¾ cups bone broth of your choice (Chapter 3)
2 tablespoons molasses
1 tablespoon freshly squeezed lemon juice
1 tablespoon apple cider vinegar
1 teaspoon cayenne pepper, or more if you prefer

1. In a small saucepan, heat the broth to a simmer.

2. Combine the molasses, lemon juice, apple cider vinegar, and cayenne pepper in a mug. Fill the mug with the broth and serve.

Master Tonic Broth

Serves 1
(plus 1 pint
Master Tonic)

PREP
20 minutes (plus
14 days resting time)

COOK
5 minutes

▶ Save the leftover
vegetables from mak-
ing the Master Tonic
in your refrigerator
and use as needed to
season various dishes.
They're great for spic-
ing up soups, adding
flavor to sautéed
greens, and bringing
heat to marinades.

Sometimes referred to as "fire cider," a mixture of jalapeños, garlic, horseradish, white onions, and ginger is steeped in apple cider vinegar for a period of 14 days. These spicy ingredients contain antibacterial, antiviral, antimicrobial, antifungal, and anti-inflammatory properties. I cannot say enough good things about this tincture. You can take shots of it when you're not feeling well, or drink it as broth. You can even mix it with olive oil and use it as a dressing on greens.

FOR THE MASTER TONIC
¾ cup stemmed and seeded jalapeños
¾ cup coarsely chopped white onion
¾ cup coarsely chopped fresh ginger
¾ cup peeled and chopped fresh horseradish
¾ cup peeled garlic cloves
2 cups apple cider vinegar

FOR THE MASTER TONIC BROTH
1¾ cups bone broth of your choice (Chapter 3)
Celtic sea salt

TO MAKE THE MASTER TONIC

1. In a food processor, process the jalapeños until they are chopped into small pieces. Add the onions and pulse. Add the ginger and pulse. Add the horseradish and pulse. Add the garlic and pulse.

2. Transfer the contents of the food processor to a quart jar and pack down firmly. Fill the jar with the apple cider vinegar. Cover the jar and store in a cool, dark place for 14 days, shaking the jar daily.

3. After 14 days, strain the mixture, reserving the liquid. Transfer 1 ounce of the liquid to a large mug, and store the rest in a glass jar for later use. It will keep in a cool, dark cabinet for up to a year.

TO MAKE THE MASTER TONIC BROTH

1. In a small saucepan, heat the broth to a simmer.

2. Pour the broth into the mug with the Master Tonic, and add a pinch of sea salt. Serve.

Energy/Weight-Loss Broth

Serves 1

PREP
5 minutes

COOK
5 minutes (plus 10 to 15 minutes steeping time)

▶ If you do not have an herb shop in your city, the easiest way to buy herbs such as ginseng is from a reputable dealer online. See Resources (page 200), for some good sources of high-quality herbs.

There are lots of spices that support weight loss, and they make you feel good, too! These spices have strong flavors; they are sweet, hot, and spicy and really add some zing to any bone broth you like. Keeping hydrated, and drinking frequently, is important when you are looking for more energy or are on a weight-loss plan. This drink with no sweeteners will help satisfy both your body's need for hydration and your sweet tooth.

1¾ cups neutral bone broth of your choice (page 38)
1½ teaspoons pastured butter, ghee, tallow, or lard
½ teaspoon ground ginseng
½ teaspoon ground cinnamon
¼ teaspoon ground turmeric
¼ teaspoon ground ginger
⅛ teaspoon ground cardamom

1. In a small saucepan, heat the broth to a simmer.

2. In a large mug, combine all the remaining ingredients. Pour the broth into the mug. Cover and steep for 10 to 15 minutes. Serve.

Stomach Soother

Serves 1

PREP
5 minutes

COOK
5 minutes (plus 10 to 15 minutes steeping time)

There is nothing more uncomfortable than having an upset stomach. Whether it's from a virus, something bad that you ate, or an overindulgence—this soothing tonic can help you feel better. It includes peppermint to soothe nausea and provide pain relief, bitters to improve digestion, and ginger for nausea and inflammation. I recommend you make this broth with a neutral, ginger-based broth for added relief.

1¾ cups neutral bone broth of your choice (page 38)
1 teaspoon apple cider vinegar
2 fresh peppermint sprigs, muddled, or 1 peppermint tea bag
4 dashes bitters
1 tablespoon minced fresh ginger or 1 teaspoon ground ginger

1. In a small saucepan, heat the broth to a simmer.

2. In a large mug, combine the remaining ingredients. Pour the broth into the mug, cover, and allow to steep for 10 to 15 minutes. Remove the peppermint sprigs (or tea bag) and the fresh ginger, and serve.

Beautiful Skin Broth

Serves 1

PREP
5 minutes

COOK
5 minutes (plus 10 to 15 minutes steeping time)

▶ If you don't have access to fresh thyme, you can substitute 1 tablespoon dried thyme. For even further healing, add an extra scoop of organic grass-fed collagen to this broth.

I designed this tonic to help fight the causes of acne as well as the effects of it from the inside out. Bone broth is combined with thyme, which has antibacterial qualities; aloe vera juice, which helps reduce inflammation; and coriander oil, which is antimicrobial. This is an excellent broth to drink along with the following recipe for Bone Broth and Green Juice to maintain optimal skin health.

1¾ cups neutral bone broth of your choice (page 38)
2 thyme sprigs, muddled
2 tablespoons aloe vera juice
1 teaspoon coriander or cilantro oil
Pinch Celtic sea salt

1. In a small saucepan, heat the broth to a simmer.

2. In a large mug, combine the remaining ingredients. Pour the broth into the mug. Cover and steep for 10 to 15 minutes. Remove the thyme and serve.

Bone Broth and Green Juice

Serves 2

PREP
15 minutes

COOK
5 minutes

▶ You can add a cold neutral bone broth to your green juice for a refreshing drink in the hot summer months. I like to use non-gelled broth for cold drinks.

I absolutely love drinking a cup of bone broth followed by a green juice in the morning. When I am on this morning regimen, my skin absolutely glows, and my hair doubles in thickness. This is also a great combination to keep hunger at bay. If I drink bone broth or green juice on its own, I usually find myself hungry about 20 minutes later, but drinking them in tandem keeps me sated for hours.

1 head romaine lettuce
1 cup kale
1 cup dandelion greens
1 cup spinach
1 cup parsley
1 large cucumber
1 large apple, cored
1 lemon, peeled
1¾ cups bone broth of your choice (Chapter 3)

1. Juice the vegetables and fruits in a juicer, and transfer to the refrigerator to chill.

2. In a small saucepan, heat the broth to a simmer.

3. Pour the hot broth into a mug and serve. When done, follow with the green juice served over ice.

Thyroid Support Broth

Serves 1

PREP
5 minutes

COOK
5 minutes (plus 10 to 15 minutes steeping time)

▶ Add a squeeze of lemon to this beverage for added zing.

Thyroid issues can range from fatigue, weight gain or loss, frequent cold or flu symptoms, lack of focus, and depression. Consumption of fish broth is an excellent way to give your thyroid a boost, as fish broth contains a high level of iodine, a key element in thyroid function that is largely missing from our modern diets. The addition of kelp or dulse provides greater iodine support to this broth, while coconut oil can give you an energy boost.

1¾ cups Fish Bone Broth (page 56) or Shellfish Broth (page 58)
¼ cup seaweed, kelp, or dulse
1 teaspoon coconut oil
¼ teaspoon Celtic sea salt

1. In a small saucepan, heat the broth to a simmer.

2. In a large mug, combine the remaining ingredients. Pour the broth into the mug, cover, and steep for 10 to 15 minutes. Serve.

Dreamy Broth

Serves 1

PREP
5 minutes

COOK
5 minutes (plus 10 to 15 minutes steeping time)

▶ This broth does double-duty as a skin-beautifying tonic. Try it out, and give your skin a treat while this natural sedative provides a welcome night's sleep. Rest assured you'll wake up looking and feeling your absolute best.

We all struggle with sleep issues from time to time. Sleep is integral to our bodies' proper functioning, so I designed this tonic to allow your body to fall asleep naturally so you can get a good night's rest. It contains chamomile, which is widely used for its calming effects; lavender oil, which has been shown to put you in a relaxed state; and ginger, which can also affect your overall mood and anxiety levels.

1¾ cups neutral bone broth of your choice (page 38)
1 chamomile tea bag
2 to 3 drops essential lavender oil
1 thin slice fresh ginger

1. In a small saucepan, heat the broth to a simmer.

2. In a large mug, combine the chamomile tea bag, lavender oil, and ginger. Pour the broth into the mug, cover, and steep for 10 to 15 minutes. Serve.

BEVERAGES

As I mentioned earlier, a mug of bone broth has become the ultimate comfort for me. But sometimes my cravings call for more than a simple broth tea. That's where this chapter comes in. Creative, refreshing, and soothing, these are quick and easy drink recipes to add to your repertoire. I've rounded out the chapter with four boozy "brothtails." While I don't advocate making a cocktail every time you want to enjoy bone broth, it can hit the spot for a special occasion. If you don't care for a gelatinous texture when you're drinking cold beverages, this would be a good time to use a batch of neutral bone broth that didn't gel (page 38). Broth that has gelled has a tendency to gel back up when in cold drinks.

Arnold Palmer in the Weeds

Serves 6

PREP
10 minutes (plus at least 30 minutes resting time)

▶ Do not add more than 1 tablespoon dried lavender, or your beverage will have a soapy taste.

A combination of bone broth, iced tea, and lavender lemonade, this is by far one of my favorite drinks. It's cool, refreshing, and easy to make and store in the refrigerator. You can make your favorite antioxidant tea or buy unsweetened antioxidant iced tea from the store. Enjoy this sweet, refreshing drink, and reap the benefits of bone broth, antioxidant tea, raw honey, and apple cider vinegar.

5½ cups iced tea
1 tablespoon dried culinary lavender
1 cup raw honey
2 cups boiling water
1 cup freshly squeezed lemon juice
1 cup cold water
1 cup chilled neutral bone broth of your choice (page 38),
   non-gelled, if desired
½ cup apple cider vinegar
Fresh mint sprigs or lavender wands, for garnish

1. Pour the iced tea into a pitcher and transfer to the refrigerator to chill.

2. Put the lavender in another pitcher or a large measuring glass. Muddle it with the back of a spoon to release some of its oils. Add the honey. Pour the boiling water over the mixture and set it aside to cool for at least 30 minutes or up to 4 hours.

3. Strain the cooled lavender mixture into the pitcher with the iced tea. Add the lemon juice, cold water, bone broth, and apple cider vinegar. Stir to combine.

4. Fill 6 highball glasses with ice, and fill with the tea-lemonade-broth mixture. Garnish with the fresh mint or lavender and serve.

Detox Broth

Serves 1

PREP
5 minutes

COOK
5 minutes (plus 5 to
7 minutes steeping
time)

▶ Instead of using
separate dandelion and
milk thistle tea bags,
look for a detoxifying
tea with dandelion,
milk thistle, and
other cleansing herb
combinations at your
local health food store
or online.

The combination of bone broth and herbal tea can help you feel great. If you'd like to "reset" your system, this recipe will incorporate detoxifying ingredients into your daily broth ritual. Dandelion and milk thistle are both known for their detoxifying and liver-friendly properties, while peppermint is renowned for its ability to soothe. You'll find both teas in health food stores.

1¾ cups neutral bone broth of your choice (page 38)
2 peppermint sprigs
1 dandelion tea bag
1 milk thistle tea bag

1. In a small saucepan, bring the bone broth to a simmer.

2. Meanwhile, in a large mug, muddle the peppermint sprigs with a pestle.

3. Pour the broth over the peppermint in the mug. Add the tea bags and steep for 5 to 7 minutes. Remove the tea bags and serve.

The Cinnamon Roll

Serves 1

PREP
5 minutes

COOK
5 minutes

▶ To make this beverage more filling, add a slice of apple for an apple pie–like treat.

I created this recipe one holiday season while experimenting with making a bone broth apple pie. After I put the pie together, I was left with a sweet and buttery apple cinnamon bone broth liquid. Not surprisingly, it was delicious. Shortly thereafter I started drinking my morning bone broth with cinnamon, a tad of sweetener, and a pat of butter, and the Cinnamon Roll was born.

1¾ cups neutral bone broth of your choice (page 38)
1 teaspoon ground cinnamon
1½ teaspoons raw honey or stevia
1 pat pastured butter

1. In a small saucepan, heat the bone broth to a simmer.

2. Combine the remaining ingredients in a large mug. Pour the hot broth into the mug and stir until the butter melts. Serve.

Cranberry-Orange Bone Broth Sparkler

Serves 6

PREP
5 minutes

▶ Serve this sparkler from a glass pitcher garnished with long stems of fragrant mint and sliced orange rounds.

How lucky we are that oranges are in season in the winter when our immune systems are at their most vulnerable! I grew up drinking variations of this cranberry and orange juice drink when I was sick and crave it to this day if I am feeling under the weather. This sparkling concoction is also a festive nonalcoholic option for holiday entertaining. For a boozy version, feel free to add vodka or gin.

2 cups sparkling mineral water

1¾ cups chilled neutral bone broth of your choice (page 38),
   non-gelled, if desired

1 cup cranberry juice cocktail

1 cup freshly squeezed orange juice

1 tablespoon apple cider vinegar

Pour all the ingredients into a large pitcher and stir to combine.

Green Bone Broth Smoothie

Serves 2

20 minutes

▶ If you prefer, you can juice this recipe instead of making it into a smoothie. Just omit the almond and coconut butter and enjoy them on a piece of toast instead! For a smoothie, simply feed the vegetables, fruits, and herbs into a juicer, and then mix this fresh green juice with the coconut water, bone broth, and apple cider vinegar.

Whenever I have a long workday ahead of me, I like to get ready by drinking one of these smoothies. It's chock-full of vitamins and minerals from fruits and vegetables, with a high fiber content that will keep you feeling full for hours. The coconut water contains beneficial sugars, electrolytes, and minerals to keep you hydrated, while the coconut butter gives you an extended energy boost. Meanwhile, the almond butter adds protein to help keep your blood sugar stable, and is also a source of healthy fat.

1 cup stemmed kale

½ cup spinach

1 cup peeled, seeded, chopped cucumber

1 large apple, cored

¼ cup mango chunks or ½ banana

½ cup apple cider vinegar

Leaves from 2 mint sprigs

1 tablespoon coconut butter

2 tablespoons almond butter

½ cup coconut water

½ cup chilled neutral bone broth of your choice (page 38), non-gelled, if desired

1. Combine the kale, spinach, cucumber, apple, mango or banana, apple cider vinegar, and mint in a blender and process on high.

2. Add the coconut butter and process until combined. Add the almond butter and process until combined. Add the coconut water and process until a creamy texture is achieved.

3. Add the bone broth and process until combined. If needed, adjust the amount of almond or coconut butter for a chunkier texture, or add additional bone broth or coconut water if the smoothie is too thick. Serve.

Wake-Up Juice

Serves 1

PREP
10 minutes

▶ Alone, this drink is crisp and bright. However, for some extra kick, add a pinch of cayenne or any other mild to hot ground chile to liven things up a bit.

I love this fruit and veggie juice, which contains the added benefits of bone broth and will leave you feeling vivacious and full. It's best consumed right away, when the vitamins and minerals in the produce are at their optimum levels. Always remember to use organic produce when you're juicing. If you can't buy all organic, all the time, refer to the Dirty Dozen and the Clean Fifteen lists (page 198) that indicate which produce has the most and least chemical residue.

1 apple, cored
1 lemon, rind removed
½ large cucumber, peeled
½ cup fresh mint leaves
½ cup fresh basil leaves
1¾ cups chilled neutral bone broth of your choice (page 38),
   non-gelled, if desired

In a juicer, process the apple, lemon, cucumber, mint, and basil. Add ice to a glass, pour in the bone broth, add the juice, and stir thoroughly. Serve.

Hot Chocolate

Makes 4 drinks

PREP
5 minutes

COOK
5 minutes

▶ For a spicy kick, add half a teaspoon of cayenne to the first step of this recipe.

Hot chocolate harkens memories of childhood—and for those of us who grew up in the '80s, microwavable packets. This recipe uses traditional methods, calling for neutral bone broth, raw milk, and raw cream. Coconut milk and coconut cream offer a delicious dairy-free option, while coconut sugar, which has a low glycemic index of 35, is a great option for those watching their sugar intake.

⅓ cup unsweetened cocoa powder
¾ cup raw cane sugar or ¾ cup of coconut sugar
1 pinch Celtic sea salt
⅓ cup boiling neutral bone broth of your choice (page 38)
3½ cups raw whole milk or coconut milk
½ cup raw cream or coconut cream
¼ teaspoon vanilla extract
Whipped cream, marshmallows, or chocolate chips, for garnish (optional)

1. In a medium saucepan, combine the cocoa, sugar, and salt.

2. Carefully add the boiling bone broth. Turn on the heat to medium and bring the entire mixture to a gentle simmer. Stir until combined for 1 to 2 minutes. Be sure not to let it scorch or burn.

3. Turn down the heat to low and add the milk to the pan, allowing the mixture to become hot but not boil.

4. Remove the pan from the heat and stir in the vanilla. Add the cream and whisk to combine.

5. Pour the mixture equally into 4 mugs. Garnish with a dollop of whipped cream, marshmallows, or chocolate chips, if using.

Ice Pick

Serves 1

PREP
5 minutes

This is one of my favorite beverage choices, based on an actual cocktail combining iced tea and vodka. It's a great brunch cocktail, and so simple to make. For a sweeter tea with antibacterial and antiviral properties, add a spoonful of raw honey.

1 ounce vodka
1 cup chilled neutral bone broth of your choice (page 38),
   non-gelled, if desired
1 cup cold iced tea
2 tablespoons apple cider vinegar Raw honey (optional) 1 mint sprig, for garnish

1. Fill a large glass with ice. Pour the vodka into the glass.

2. Add the bone broth, iced tea, and apple cider vinegar.

3. If desired, add up to 1 teaspoon honey for sweetness.

4. Stir well, garnish with mint, and serve.

The Mexican Ginger

Serves 1

PREP
5 minutes

Margarita, anyone? This juicy cocktail combines citrus, bitters, ginger ale, and tequila with bone broth. The strong flavors of lime, honey, and orange bitters mask the flavor of the bone broth so you barely know it's there. If you're not a fan of tequila, substituting vodka or gin works just fine. If you prefer, it can also be made without alcohol.

1¾ cups chilled neutral bone broth of your choice (page 38), non-gelled, if desired

3 tablespoons freshly squeezed orange juice

2 tablespoons freshly squeezed lime juice

½ teaspoon apple cider vinegar

1 teaspoon raw honey

4 dashes orange bitters

1 ounce tequila

1½ cups ginger ale

Lime wedge, for garnish

1. Fill a shaker with ice cubes. Add the bone broth, orange juice, lime juice, apple cider vinegar, honey, and orange bitters.

2. Shake and strain into a tumbler glass filled with ice cubes. Add the tequila to the glass.

3. Top off with the ginger ale. Garnish with a lime wedge and serve.

Grandpa's Cough Medicine

Serves 1 drink

PREP
5 minutes

COOK
5 minutes
(plus 5 minutes
steeping time)

▶ If you prefer to make
this as a cold cocktail,
use 2 to 3 drops of
essential thyme oil and
a chilled neutral bone
broth (non-gelled, if
desired).

This drink has a cheeky name, but I designed the recipe with health and healing in mind. The raw honey soothes the sorest of throats and can loosen congestion, while acting as an antiviral agent. Thyme has long been used to calm coughing, and its properties have been said to help fight bronchitis. The Meyer lemons add an extra level of sweetness while at the same time helping to prevent dehydration. Finally, the whiskey adds flavor and is a traditional addition to cold and cough toddies.

1¾ cups neutral bone broth of your choice (page 38)
1 tablespoon fresh or 1 teaspoon dried thyme
Juice of ½ Meyer lemon
1 lemon slice
1½ teaspoons raw honey
1 ounce whiskey

1. In a small saucepan, heat the bone broth to a simmer.

2. Combine the remaining ingredients in a large mug. Pour the hot broth into the mug. Cover and allow to steep for 5 minutes. Uncover, stir, and enjoy.

Bloody Mary

Serves 8

PREP

10 minutes (plus at least 2 hours resting time)

▶ Use fish or shellfish broth to create a refreshing and iodine-rich *cóctel de mariscos*, a Mexican staple and one of my favorite drinks. Use beer instead of vodka, and garnish with shrimp, crab, and clams. For a party, set up a Bloody Mary bar for your guests with extras like hot sauce, hot peppers, pickled vegetables, and cooked bacon strips.

Long before I ever had a clue about bone broth, I always added a dash of chicken stock to my Sunday bloody—I love the deep flavor a meaty broth can add. Based on the classic brunch cocktail, this Bloody Mary is equally great after a workout or long run. If you're making this in the summer, don't be afraid to juice your own tomatoes! There are so many varieties these days—your bloody doesn't have to be red. You can choose from yellow, orange, or green. A lot of heirloom varieties offer an amazing level of sweetness as well as a smoky flavor.

2 cups tomato juice

1 cup chilled neutral bone broth of your choice (page 38), non-gelled, if desired

3 tablespoons apple cider vinegar

3 tablespoons lime juice

1 tablespoon Worcestershire sauce

2 to 4 tablespoons grated fresh horseradish

1 tablespoon grated fresh ginger

1½ teaspoons hot sauce

2 teaspoons freshly cracked black pepper

1 teaspoon celery seed

1 teaspoon Celtic sea salt

8 ounces vodka, divided

Celery sticks and/or olives, for garnish

1. In a nonreactive pitcher, combine all the ingredients except the vodka and garnishes and allow to sit for 2 to 24 hours for the flavors to combine. When ready to serve, mix thoroughly.

2. Add ice to 8 glasses. Pour 1 ounce vodka into each glass. Top each glass with the tomato juice mixture.

3. Garnish with celery sticks or olives, as desired.

CHAPTER 5

MORNING
PICK-ME-UPS

We've all heard that breakfast is the most important meal of the day. Here you'll find a variety of recipes to ensure that your day starts off right. Ranging from your typical breakfast foods to those that are a bit more unexpected, all of these morning meals use bone broth to pack an extra wellness punch. Included are some of my personal favorite breakfast go-to's as well as dishes great for entertaining the brunch crowd.

Asian Breakfast Bowl

Serves 1

PREP
5 minutes

COOK
15 minutes (plus 10 minutes resting time)

▶ You can add any vegetables to this dish by following the seasonal veggie guide (page 197).

Start your day in a spicy way! This is a great breakfast to get you going on a cold morning. The recipe uses seasonal vegetables with the addition of egg to provide omega-3 fatty acids and protein. Consider adding fish sauce or bonito flakes for a more complex flavor. Adding fermented or spiced ingredients such as gochujang, sambal, or kimchi is also tasty and can add probiotic benefits to the dish. Be creative!

1 egg
1¾ cups bone broth of your choice (Chapter 3)
1 cup cooked rice noodles
½ avocado, sliced
¼ cup thinly sliced tomato
¼ cup thinly sliced peeled cucumber
4 to 5 thin jalapeño slices

1. Bring a small saucepan of water to a boil. Use a spoon to gently lower the egg into the water. Set a timer for 6 minutes. When it's finished, run the egg under cold water, peel, cut it in half, and set aside.

2. Pour out the water from the saucepan and add the bone broth. Heat the bone broth to a simmer. Remove the pan from the heat.

3. Put the noodles in a bowl and add all the vegetables. Pour the broth into the bowl, add the egg halves, cover, and allow to sit for 10 minutes. Serve.

Poached Egg in Bone Broth with Sweet Potato and Kale

Serves 1

PREP
5 minutes

COOK
15 minutes (plus 5 minutes resting time)

▶ Add any other greens such as chard, arugula, or baby collards greens, or other vegetables such as squash, sweet peas, or corn, for a fiber-rich breakfast.

This recipe offers an easy solution for everyday breakfast. It's low in calories, so it's ideal if you are trying to lose weight. I like to poach sweet potatoes in bone broth and store them in the refrigerator—they keep for up to a week. High in fiber and rich in beta-carotene, sweet potatoes are Paleo-friendly and great for maintaining healthy blood sugar levels.

1¾ cups bone broth of your choice (Chapter 3)
1 teaspoon apple cider vinegar
1 egg
4 thin sweet potato slices
1 cup chopped kale
Celtic sea salt
Freshly ground black pepper

1. In a small pan, bring the bone broth to a simmer. Add the apple cider vinegar.

2. Crack the egg into the broth gently so that it remains intact. Use a spoon to cradle the white of the egg once or twice to keep it together as it cooks. Cook for 5 to 6 minutes, as desired. Remove the egg using a slotted spoon, cover to keep warm, and set aside.

3. Add the sweet potato slices to the broth, and poach until just fork-tender, 4 to 5 minutes.

4. Put the kale in a bowl. Top the kale with the sweet potato slices and poached egg. Pour the hot poaching broth over all. Cover and allow to stand for 5 to 7 minutes. Season with salt and pepper and serve.

Zucchini Power Pancakes

Makes 6 pancakes
(serves 3)

PREP
20 minutes

COOK
25 minutes

▶ Make a peanut butter and banana power pancake sandwich by adding your favorite nut butter and sliced banana.

I created this recipe out of sheer necessity—something had to be done with all the extra zucchini in my garden. One day I decided to try my hand at creating a bone broth–rich power pancake with the flavor of zucchini quick bread, enhanced by lightly toasted walnuts and the classic spices, cinnamon and nutmeg. Perfect for freezing, these pancakes can easily be reheated for breakfasts on the go.

1 cup grated zucchini
Pinch plus ¼ teaspoon Celtic sea salt, divided
1 cup roughly chopped raw walnuts
¾ cup neutral bone broth of your choice (page 38)
¼ cup coconut milk
1 egg
2 tablespoons melted pastured butter, ghee,
 or coconut oil, plus more for greasing the pan
2 teaspoons raw cane sugar
¼ teaspoon ground cinnamon
⅛ teaspoon ground nutmeg
⅛ teaspoon ground turmeric
1½ cups whole-wheat flour or gluten-free flour
½ teaspoon baking powder
¼ teaspoon baking soda

1. Toss the zucchini in a colander with a pinch of salt, and allow to sit for 10 minutes. After 10 minutes, lay the zucchini on a clean dish towel or paper towel, and roll it up to wring out the excess water.

2. Heat a small skillet over medium-high heat and toast the walnuts until there is a faint yet rich walnut aroma, 3 to 5 minutes. Do not allow them to burn. Immediately transfer the walnuts to a cool plate and set aside to cool.

3. In a large mixing bowl, mix the bone broth, coconut milk, egg, butter, cane sugar, cinnamon, nutmeg, and turmeric.

4. Add the flour, baking powder, baking soda, and remaining ¼ teaspoon of salt. Mix well.

5. Fold the zucchini into the batter, and then fold the walnuts into the batter.

6. Lightly grease a large frying pan or griddle with a small amount of butter, ghee, or coconut oil. Heat the pan over medium-high heat.

7. Add ¼ cup of the batter to the pan for each pancake. Cook the pancakes until they become crispy around the edges and bubbles form on the surface.

8. Using a spatula, flip the pancakes and allow them to thoroughly cook through until they are firm and crisp, about 5 minutes more.

9. Serve immediately, or keep warm in a 200°F oven until serving time.

Sprouted Brown Rice and Eggs

Serves 1

PREP
10 minutes

COOK
20 minutes

▶ Having sprouted rice on hand made with bone broth is a great freezer staple. Once you've prepared a batch, simply freeze it in measured packages, and use it for quick stir-fries and soups.

This breakfast leaves you feeling very full and very happy! Using a small dash of fish sauce adds a really nice depth of saltiness but doesn't leave you with a fishy flavor. I like to cook my veggies for this dish in a generous amount of tallow or lard. Cooking them at a high heat allows them to develop a nice flavorful sear, while keeping their crunch and firmness on the inside.

1 cup uncooked sprouted brown rice (page 93)
1½ cups plus 1 tablespoon bone broth of your choice (Chapter 3), divided
2½ teaspoons tallow, lard, or poultry fat, divided
1 cup diced summer squash
½ cup shredded cooked meat of your choice (optional)
2 eggs
2 dashes fish sauce, plus more for serving (optional)
½ cup shredded roasted, salted seaweed

1. Cook the sprouted rice in 1½ cups of the bone broth according to the package instructions, keeping in mind that the rice has already absorbed a lot of moisture, so the cook time will be shorter than usual.

2. Meanwhile, in a medium skillet, heat 1½ teaspoons of the tallow over medium heat. Add the summer squash and sauté until fork-tender, 3 to 5 minutes. Transfer the squash to a plate and set aside. Add the meat (if using) and heat thoroughly, and then transfer to the same plate with the squash.

3. In a small bowl, beat the eggs with the remaining 1 tablespoon bone broth and the fish sauce (if using). Heat the remaining 1 teaspoon tallow in the same skillet. Scramble the eggs over medium heat until fluffy.

4. Scoop the cooked rice into a bowl and top it with the squash, eggs, and meat. Scatter the seaweed over all. Serve with fish sauce (if using).

SOAKING AND SPROUTING BROWN RICE

Soaking and sprouting brown rice allows your body to easily digest the grain itself as well as making the nutrients more bioavailable to your system. When you soak and sprout brown rice (or any grains or legumes), you are removing the gluten, lectin, and phytic acid that can cause digestive upsets. Just follow these steps, which can be adapted for any grains or legumes.

1. Rinse your organic brown rice in a colander and transfer to a glass jar or bowl. Add enough warm filtered water to completely cover the rice.

2. Loosely cover the jar or bowl with a towel and set aside in a warm area of the kitchen for about 12 hours.

3. Pour the rice back into the colander and drain the soaking liquid. Rinse well with fresh water, and shake off any excess moisture.

4. Leave the rice in the colander set over a bowl, covered loosely with a towel, and repeat the rinsing and draining process 2 or 3 times per day. After 1 or 2 days you will begin to see a very tiny sprout emerge from the ends of the grains of rice. You don't want the rice to sprout any more than this.

5. Use the rice right away or store it in the refrigerator until you're ready to use (if storing in the refrigerator, make sure that it is not sitting in any excess liquid).

Keep in mind when you are cooking sprouted rice that the amount of water or bone broth needed will be less than what's called for in the package directions because the grains have already absorbed quite a bit of moisture. The cook time will also be shorter, so keep an eye on it while it's cooking.

Chilaquiles with Summer Squash

Serves 8 to 10

PREP
10 minutes

COOK
40 minutes

Chilaquiles is a traditional Mexican dish and an ingenious way to use left-over tortillas. Frying the tortillas in beef tallow lends an amazing flavor. Seasonal vegetables, fermented salsa, and two kinds of cheese make this a hearty and satisfying meal any time of day. I like to serve this dish with a pot of robust beans cooked in bone broth, along with a refreshing salad.

2 cups tallow
30 (6-inch) corn tortillas, torn into strips
¼ cup chopped onion
1 cup chopped summer squash
8 eggs, lightly beaten
½ cup bone broth of your choice (Chapter 3)
1 cup fermented salsa or regular salsa, divided
½ cup cotija cheese (optional)
½ cup shredded raw Jack cheese (optional)

1. Preheat the oven to 375°F.

2. In a large, deep pot, heat the tallow to 375°F.

3. Add the tortilla strips to the hot oil and fry until crisp, 3 to 5 minutes. Remove with tongs and drain on a plate lined with paper towels.

4. Transfer 1 teaspoon of the hot tallow to a large skillet and heat over medium-high heat. Sauté the onion until it is translucent, and then add the squash to the pan. Sauté until the squash is fork-tender, another 3 to 5 minutes.

5. Put the tortilla strips in a large baking dish. Top with the sautéed vegetables and toss to combine.

6. In a small bowl, mix the beaten eggs, bone broth, and ½ cup of the salsa. Pour this mixture over the tortillas and vegetables. Sprinkle with the cheese, if using.

7. Bake until the eggs are set and the cheese (if using) is melted and golden brown, 20 to 25 minutes. Serve with the remaining ½ cup salsa.

Spiced Sweet Potato Pancakes with Toasted Pecans

Makes 6 pancakes (serves 3)

PREP
30 minutes

COOK
25 minutes

▶ These pancakes are perfect for freezing and can be reheated easily for breakfasts on the go. To store, transfer the cooled pancakes to a resealable bag or container and freeze for up to 1 month.

These pancakes are wonderful in the fall when sweet potatoes are in season. Sweet potatoes are an excellent vegetable to include in your morning routine, and the aromatic spices are rich and warming. By only lightly toasting raw pecans, you retain more of their nutritional value, and by replacing the milk that these recipes usually call for, with bone broth and coconut milk, the result is a nutritious and dairy-free pancake.

1 cup thinly sliced sweet potatoes

¾ cup neutral bone broth of your choice (page 38)

1 cup roughly chopped raw pecans

1 egg, lightly beaten

¼ cup coconut milk

2 tablespoons melted pastured butter, ghee, or coconut oil, plus more for greasing the pan

2 teaspoons raw cane sugar

½ teaspoon ground turmeric

½ teaspoon cayenne pepper

⅛ teaspoon ground cinnamon

1½ cups whole-wheat flour or gluten-free flour

½ teaspoon baking powder

¼ teaspoon baking soda

¼ teaspoon Celtic sea salt

1. Combine the sweet potato slices and bone broth in a small saucepan. Bring to a simmer over medium heat and cook until the sweet potatoes are completely fork-tender, for 10 to 15 minutes. Transfer the sweet potatoes to a small bowl and smash them with a fork until they are almost completely smooth.

2. Heat a small skillet over medium-high heat and add the pecans. Toast the pecans until there is a faint, yet rich pecan aroma, 3 to 5 minutes. Do not allow them to burn. Immediately transfer the pecans to a cool plate and set aside to cool. ▶

Spiced Sweet Potato Pancakes
with Toasted Pecans continued

3. In a medium bowl, combine the egg, coconut milk, butter or oil, sugar, turmeric, cayenne, and cinnamon. Mix well. Stir in the flour, baking powder, baking soda, and salt.

4. Fold in the mashed sweet potatoes, and stir until incorporated throughout, leaving your batter slightly lumpy and a continuous rich orange color. Fold in the lightly toasted pecans, and mix until incorporated.

5. Lightly grease a large frying pan or griddle with a small amount of butter, ghee, or coconut oil, and heat over medium-high heat.

6. Add ¼ cup batter to the pan for each pancake. When the edges become golden brown and bubbles form on the surface, they are ready to be flipped.

7. Using a spatula, flip the pancake and continue to cook on the other side until firm and crisp, about 5 more minutes.

8. Serve immediately, or keep warm in a 200°F oven until serving time.

Seasonal Frittata

Serves 6 to 8

PREP
10 minutes

COOK
30 minutes

▶ A frittata is a great place to be creative with leftovers. Some of my favorite combinations for a frittata are tomato, basil, and mozzarella; mushroom, onion, ham, and Swiss cheese; or sweet potato, kale, scallions, and short rib meat.

Italian omelets, or frittatas, are satisfying for lunch, brunch, or a light dinner and can be served hot, at room temperature, or cold. They are also a great way to clean out your refrigerator or turn leftovers into an entirely new meal. There's really no wrong answer as to what ingredients you can or cannot put in a frittata, so let your imagination go wild.

2 teaspoons tallow, divided
1 cup diced seasonal vegetables
8 eggs
¼ cup bone broth of your choice (Chapter 3)
¼ cup raw whole milk or heavy cream (optional)
1 cup diced cooked bacon, ham, beef, or chicken
½ cup shredded raw cheese (optional)

1. Preheat the oven to 350°F.

2. In a large cast-iron skillet, heat 1 teaspoon of the tallow over medium-high heat. Sauté the vegetables until fork-tender, 5 to 7 minutes.

3. Meanwhile, in a large bowl, beat the eggs, bone broth, and milk or cream (if using) until combined.

4. Transfer the sautéed vegetables to the bowl with the egg mixture. Add the meat and cheese (if using) and stir to combine.

5. Heat the remaining 1 teaspoon tallow in the same skillet over medium heat. Pour the egg mixture into the skillet and cook the frittata until the edges just begin to set, 5 to 7 minutes.

6. Transfer the skillet to the oven and bake until completely set, 16 to 18 minutes. Cut into wedges and serve.

Breakfast Salad

Serves 2

PREP
10 minutes

COOK
25 minutes

▶ To make a heartier meal, or if you prefer to omit the pork, cook a piece of wild salmon to top the salad instead. The heart-healthy salmon makes a great accompaniment to the creamy richness of the potatoes.

This salad has all the elements of a classic breakfast: potatoes, eggs, and bacon. However, you can eat it any time of day—it makes a terrific one-dish lunch or light dinner. The potatoes are cooked twice, first in bone broth and then in tallow. Cooking potatoes in any liquid other than water is an effective technique for adding flavor and richness.

2 cups bone broth of your choice (Chapter 3)
1 cup sliced (lengthwise) fingerling potatoes
4 slices thick-cut European-style bacon or ham
¼ cup tallow
2 tablespoons olive oil
1 tablespoon apple cider vinegar
2 teaspoons Dijon mustard
2 cups mixed bitter, spicy greens (such as arugula and/or frisée)
2 eggs

1. In a large pot, bring the bone broth to a simmer. Add the potatoes and cook until just fork-tender, 5 to 7 minutes. Drain the potatoes and set aside.

2. Heat a large skillet over medium-high heat, and cook the bacon or ham, flipping once or twice until cooked through. Transfer to a plate lined with paper towels and set aside.

3. In the same skillet, heat the tallow. Add the potatoes to the skillet and cook until golden-brown on both sides. Remove the potatoes from the pan and drain on another plate lined with paper towels.

4. In a large bowl, whisk together the olive oil, apple cider vinegar, and Dijon mustard. Add the mixed greens and toss to coat. Add the potatoes and toss to coat.

5. Heat the same skillet once more over medium-high heat, and crack the eggs into the pan, leaving space between them. Cook until over-easy, covering the pan for the last minute to allow the eggs to set well, 3 to 5 minutes total.

6. To serve, divide the potatoes and greens between two plates, and place half of the bacon or ham on the side. Top with the fried eggs and serve.

Roasted Bone Marrow, Egg, and Spicy Greens

Serves 1

PREP
5 minutes

COOK
20 minutes

This recipe does not include bone broth. Instead, it features bone marrow, which is a luxurious delicacy when roasted—and fondly known as "meat butter." The spicy greens not only are a nice counterpoint to this very rich dish, but also have many healthy properties. Use a small spoon or butter knife to extract the marrow from the bones and spread it on the toast.

2 (1- to 2-inch) crosscut marrowbones
½ teaspoon tallow
1 egg
1 cup spicy greens (such as mustard, arugula, and/or endive)
1 teaspoon apple cider vinegar
1 teaspoon olive oil
Celtic sea salt
Freshly ground black pepper
2 slices of bread, toasted and cut in half

1. Preheat the oven to 450°F.

2. Line a baking sheet with aluminum foil. Spread the marrowbones on the sheet and roast until well-browned and bubbly, 15 to 20 minutes.

3. In a small skillet, heat the tallow. Fry the egg, flipping once, till it's done to your liking, 3 to 5 minutes total.

4. In a small bowl, toss the greens with the vinegar and olive oil and season with salt and pepper.

5. Arrange the dressed greens on a plate alongside the marrowbones, egg, and toast. Serve.

CHAPTER 6

SAUCES AND GRAVIES

Sauces are an easy way to slip bone broth into any meal. They also promise to add a whole lot of flavor to your cooking. This chapter offers some simple ways to make delicious, nutrient-dense sauces for any occasion. Many of the sauces here use items that are likely already in your refrigerator, and I also adapted a few comfort food classics. You'll find many of the recipes here paired with other dishes throughout this book.

Citrus Seafood Sauce

Makes 1 cup

PREP
20 minutes

COOK
10 minutes

▶ For a refreshing citrusy seafood soup base, add up to 2 cups each of Chicken Bone Broth (page 41), and Fish Bone Broth (page 56) or Shellfish Broth (page 58) to this recipe, and transform your favorite seafood soup with this orange-lime combination.

Refreshing orange and lime enhance all kinds of seafood. I like to serve this sauce on salmon, opah, or yellowtail. It is also excellent for steaming shellfish, such as mussels or shrimp, or for poaching fish. To poach, simply add an extra ½ cup broth along with the sauce and shellfish or fish, and let it steam until just cooked through.

2 tablespoons pastured butter, ghee, tallow, or lard
¼ cup chopped shallots
½ cup Chicken Bone Broth (page 41)
½ cup Fish Bone Broth (page 56) or Shellfish Broth (page 58)
2 tablespoons freshly squeezed orange juice
2 tablespoons freshly squeezed lime juice
1 tablespoon apple cider vinegar
1 tablespoon raw cane sugar

1. In a small saucepan, melt the butter over medium heat. Add the shallots and cook until translucent.

2. Add the chicken and seafood broths, orange and lime juices, vinegar, and sugar, stirring to combine. Bring to a boil, and then lower the heat to simmer, reducing the sauce by one-quarter.

White Wine and Dill Sauce

Makes 1½ cups

PREP
5 minutes

COOK
5 minutes

White wine, dill, and butter are traditional seasonings for fish. Here those ingredients are combined with seafood stock and a hint of garlic to yield a light, herbal sauce. A perfect accompaniment to fish and seafood, this sauce can be served with sautéed fish or shrimp, steamed mussels or clams, or even lobster. Or try drizzling a little of the sauce on boiled or baked potatoes, or noodles.

1 cup Fish Bone Broth (page 56) or Shellfish Broth (page 58)
½ cup minced fresh dill
½ cup pastured butter, ghee, tallow, or lard
1 garlic clove, minced
1 tablespoon apple cider vinegar

1. In a small saucepan, combine the broth, dill, butter, and garlic. Slowly melt the butter or ghee over low heat.

2. Remove the pan from the heat, swirl in the apple cider vinegar, and serve immediately.

Herbed Mustard Sauce

Makes 1 cup

PREP
5 minutes

COOK
40 minutes

▶ If you prefer an even thicker consistency, continue simmering the sauce for up to 10 additional minutes before adding the honey.

Honey, fresh herbs, and mustard, along with onions and garlic, form the basis of this simple sauce that tastes like it took a lot more effort to prepare than it actually does. It's also extremely versatile. Use it as a glaze on your favorite poultry, game, or lamb; as a dipping sauce with roasted vegetables; or as a dip for chips or raw vegetables like carrots, celery, or snap peas.

1½ teaspoons pastured butter, ghee, tallow, or lard
1 onion, thinly sliced
¼ cup whole-grain mustard
2 garlic cloves, minced
1 teaspoon dried thyme
1 teaspoon dried rosemary
2 cups bone broth of your choice (Chapter 3)
2 tablespoons raw honey

1. In a large saucepan, melt the butter over medium-high heat. Add the onion and cook, stirring frequently, until softened, 8 to 10 minutes.

2. Stir in the mustard, garlic, thyme, and rosemary.

3. Add the bone broth and bring the sauce to a boil. Lower the heat to a simmer and cook, stirring occasionally, until the sauce is reduced by half, 20 to 25 minutes.

4. Add the honey to the sauce, stirring to combine. Serve.

Spicy Asian Dressing or Marinade

Makes 1 cup

PREP

10 minutes (plus at least 30 minutes chilling time)

▶ If you intend to keep this in the refrigerator as a salad dressing—that is, for longer than the 4 hours suggested for chilling—omit the cilantro and mint until you're ready to use it. Right before serving, mince the herbs and whisk them into the dressing.

I first learned about larb—a kind of cold minced meat salad—from two Laotian sisters, when we worked together at an organic farm. I immediately fell in love with its delicious flavor and now either make it or order it whenever I get the opportunity. I have designed this sauce so you can use it as a dressing for any traditional larb or as a marinade for meats, poultry, and seafood.

¼ cup freshly squeezed lime juice

¼ cup non-gelled bone broth of your choice (Chapter 3)

3 tablespoons toasted sesame oil

2 tablespoons apple cider vinegar

2 tablespoons fish sauce

2 tablespoons raw honey

1 tablespoon liquid aminos

½ teaspoon sambal

3 tablespoons minced fresh cilantro

2 tablespoons minced fresh mint

In a small bowl, whisk together all the ingredients until completely combined. Chill in the refrigerator for at least 30 minutes or up to 4 hours.

Whiskey-Fig Sauce

Makes 1½ cups

PREP
5 minutes

COOK
30 minutes

▶ This is a sauce you can make ahead of time. It will keep for a week in the refrigerator or up to 6 months in the freezer.

I created this recipe many summers ago when I had access to a fig tree laden with fruit. The sweet and savory sauce is aromatic with earthy figs and smoky whiskey. Requiring few ingredients, it's a snap to prepare. I originally used it as a grilling sauce for chicken, but it's also excellent paired with lamb, salmon, duck, or game meats.

2 cups fresh figs, peeled and quartered
1 cup bone broth of your choice (Chapter 3)
½ cup whiskey
2 teaspoons liquid aminos

In a medium saucepan, combine all the ingredients and bring to a boil over medium-high heat. Reduce the heat and simmer, stirring occasionally, until the sauce has thickened to a syrupy consistency, 25 minutes. Serve.

Sweet and Sour Peppers

Serves 4 to 6

PREP
10 minutes

COOK
20 minutes

▶ Serve these piquant peppers with grilled chicken or fish, or spoon them over goat cheese and crisp bread to make bruschetta.

Sweet and sour sauces possibly originated in the Hunan region of China, where they are usually associated with fish dishes. This version, however, hails from Italy, where it is commonly paired with pork or wild game. Use the sauce with any meat entrée; alternatively, it makes a nice addition to vegetable dishes or works as a condiment with cheeses, breads, or cured meats.

1 tablespoon tallow or lard
3 cups sliced red, yellow, and green bell peppers
1 red onion, sliced
1 white onion, sliced
1 garlic clove, minced
½ cup raisins
½ cup bone broth of your choice (Chapter 3)
¼ cup balsamic vinegar
¼ cup apple cider vinegar
3 tablespoons raw cane sugar
½ cup pine nuts

1. In a medium saucepan, melt the tallow over medium heat.

2. Add the peppers, onions, and garlic to the pan, stirring to combine. Cook the vegetables until they become soft and translucent, 10 to 15 minutes.

3. Add the raisins to the pan, stirring to combine.

4. In a small bowl, whisk together the bone broth, vinegars, and sugar. Increase the heat to high and add the liquid to the pan. Stir continuously until the sauce is reduced, thickened, and coating the vegetables.

5. Toss in the pine nuts and serve immediately.

Bourbon Fruit Chutney

Makes 1½ cups

PREP
5 minutes

COOK
30 minutes

Chutney is commonly served with meat in many countries, including England and South Africa. I personally fell in love with the combination while visiting Cape Town a few years ago. While I originally developed this recipe to accompany ostrich, I find that the sauce enhances almost any meat or poultry dish. It is richly flavored yet simple to make.

This chutney is featured in my recipe for Braised Lamb Shoulder with Preserved Lemons and Bourbon Fruit Chutney (page 176).

1 cup bone broth of your choice (Chapter 3)
¾ cup savory fruit chutney
½ cup bourbon
2 teaspoons liquid aminos

1. In a small saucepan, combine the bone broth, fruit chutney, and bourbon and stir to combine. Heat over medium-high heat, bring to a boil, and then reduce the heat to a simmer. Simmer for 15 minutes.

2. Add the liquid aminos and continue simmering until the sauce has thickened, about 15 more minutes. Serve.

Apple Butter–Ale Sauce

Makes 1½ cups

PREP
5 minutes

COOK
30 minutes

▶ For a different flavor twist, replace the apple butter in this recipe with any jam you have on hand.

This recipe is perfect for summer or fall. It's great for outdoor grilling but also for savory braised or roasted meat. The apple butter and brandy caramelize beautifully into a flavorful glaze, and finishing the sauce with a swirl of the apple cider vinegar really brightens this versatile sauce. At once a braising liquid, marinade, and barbecue glaze, this sauce will last in your refrigerator for up to a week and a half, and also freezes well.

I use this sauce for my Apple Butter and Ale Pork Ribs with Sweet Potatoes (page 182).

1 cup bone broth of your choice (Chapter 3)

1 cup ale

1 cup apple butter

½ cup orange juice

2 tablespoons brandy

1 tablespoon apple cider vinegar

½ teaspoon Celtic sea salt

1. In a small saucepan, combine the bone broth, ale, apple butter, orange juice, and brandy. Bring the mixture to a boil over medium heat, reduce the heat, and simmer until the sauce is reduced by half, about 20 minutes.

2. Remove the pan from the heat and stir in the apple cider vinegar and sea salt. Serve.

Sautéed Shiitake Mushrooms in Port Sauce

Serves 4 to 6

PREP
5 minutes

COOK
15 minutes

▶ Shiitake mushrooms have strong medicinal qualities, but so do many other mushrooms. If fresh shiitakes are not readily available to you, try using maitake or oyster mushrooms instead for a delicious alternative in this classic dish.

A port wine–mushroom sauce is a classic accompaniment to steak, but it's just as delicious with burgers, lamb, game meats, and rich pork dishes. I adapted this recipe to substitute shiitake mushrooms for conventional button mushrooms. Of course, numerous varieties of mushrooms are known for their beneficial properties, so by all means, use your favorite— just be sure to never eat wild mushrooms without a field guide and a second opinion.

1 tablespoon tallow
1 tablespoon pastured butter
2 cups sliced shiitake mushrooms
¼ cup diced white onion
2 tablespoons balsamic vinegar
1 cup bone broth of your choice (Chapter 3)
¼ cup port wine
1 tablespoon liquid aminos
½ teaspoon whole-grain mustard
1 teaspoon dried rosemary

1. In a medium saucepan, melt the tallow and butter over medium-high heat. Add the mushrooms, onion, and balsamic vinegar. Bring the mixture to a boil, scraping the sides of the pot and stirring the mixture frequently.

2. Add the bone broth, port, liquid aminos, mustard, and rosemary. Bring to a boil, reduce the heat, and simmer, stirring occasionally, until the sauce thickens, about 10 more minutes.

White Gravy

Makes 1½ cups

PREP
5 minutes

COOK
10 minutes

▶ You can adapt this recipe to meat drippings from a roast or bird. To do this, replace the tallow or lard and the butter in the recipe with equal parts of drippings from the roast or bird, and proceed with the recipe as usual.

Rich and creamy white gravy uses both milk and bone broth and is thickened with flour. I make this recipe for special occasions with friends, and love to serve it with fried chicken. The recipe calls for both tallow or lard and pastured butter, which produces an amazing flavor and a gravy that is more nutritionally beneficial. Though good-quality leaf lard may be tricky to find, it was once the most popular cooking fat in the United States and is well worth seeking out.

I always serve this gravy with Grammy Bee's Fried Chicken (page 171).

2 tablespoons tallow or lard
2 tablespoons pastured butter
¼ cup flour
¼ teaspoon Celtic sea salt
¼ teaspoon freshly ground black pepper
1½ cups raw whole milk
1 cup bone broth of your choice (Chapter 3)

1. In a small saucepan, melt the tallow and butter over low heat. Stir in the flour, salt, and pepper, stirring constantly until the mixture is smooth and bubbly.

2. Add the milk and bone broth slowly, whisking constantly as the liquids are added. Bring the gravy to a boil for 1 minute. Reduce the heat and simmer until the gravy thickens, 3 to 5 more minutes. Serve.

Spring Garden White Sauce

Makes 1 cup

PREP
10 minutes

COOK
35 minutes

▶ If your sauce is too runny, place it in a small saucepan and allow it to simmer on low heat. Stir constantly until you reach your desired thickness.

This is one of my favorite recipes. Its simple preparation and ingredients leave you with a versatile and aromatic sauce that is excellent on pizzas and pastas, and can also be cleverly used as a soup base. The key to retaining the white color is cooking the sauce on a low heat. It takes a bit of time, but I promise you, it is well worth the wait.

1 tablespoon tallow
1 cup fennel, cored and chopped
1½ cups white onion, chopped
5 cloves garlic, chopped
1 cup Chicken Bone Broth (page 41)
2–3 tablespoons olive oil
½ teaspoon Celtic sea salt
½ teaspoon white pepper
¼ teaspoon apple cider vinegar

1. In a medium saucepan on low heat, melt the tallow. Add the fennel, allowing it to cook until it becomes translucent and soft, about 5 minutes. Add the onions and cook for 7 to 10 minutes, being careful not to let anything brown or burn in the pan. Add the garlic and cook for 2 to 3 minutes.

2. Add the bone broth and bring the mixture to a simmer for about 15 minutes, or until most of the liquid has evaporated.

3. Transfer to a food processor and pulse the mixture 4 or 5 times. Turn the food processor to high and drizzle in 1 tablespoon of olive oil at a time, until the sauce becomes thick, smooth, and creamy.

4. Add the salt, pepper, and apple cider vinegar and pulse a few more times to combine. Serve immediately. Store this in the refrigerator for up to one week, or in the freezer for up to 6 months.

CHAPTER 7

SOUPS AND STEWS

When thinking about how to turn bone broth into a meal, soups and stews are probably the first dishes that come to mind. The recipes in this chapter provide fresh takes on age-old soups and stews, many of which originated in the Old World, when meals reflected the necessity of using the odd bits and ends of animals, along with whatever else may have been available. You'll also find some wonderful facts about where some of our favorite soups and stews originated, how far they've traveled, and how much some of them have changed since their early counterparts.

Cauliflower-Sambal Bisque

Serves 2

PREP
15 minutes

COOK
45 minutes

Cauliflower is my favorite vegetable, and when puréed, it makes a lovely soup that is easy to prepare and equally delicious served hot or cold. The buttery flavor of the ghee, rich bone broth, and creamy coconut milk combine to produce a dreamy texture without any added milk or cream. Spicy sambal is similar to sriracha but is usually used for cooking rather than dipping. Sambal consists of chiles, salt, lime juice or vinegar, and sugar, and can be either cooked or fermented.

4 cups cauliflower florets
1 onion, sliced
4 garlic cloves, peeled
2 cups bone broth of your choice (Chapter 3)
2 cups coconut milk
1 teaspoon sambal
3 lime leaves
1 tablespoon apple cider vinegar
1 tablespoon ghee, tallow, or lard
½ teaspoon Celtic sea salt

1. Combine the cauliflower, onion, garlic, and bone broth in a large stockpot. Heat over medium-high heat to boiling, and then reduce the heat to a simmer. Cook until the cauliflower is fork-tender, about 15 minutes.

2. Carefully transfer the contents of the pot to a food processor or blender and process until puréed. If you are using a blender, remove the center cover from the lid and hold a towel over the hole to let some steam escape. Return the purée to the pot.

3. Add the coconut milk, sambal, and lime leaves. Stir to combine.

4. Bring the mixture back to simmering, and simmer until the soup has reduced by half and is thick, about 30 minutes.

5. Stir in the apple cider vinegar, ghee, and salt. Serve.

Curried Butternut Squash

This luscious soup has a distinctly Indian accent, featuring ghee, curry, turmeric, cayenne, and coconut milk. Use your favorite commercial curry powder, or make your own. Spices that complement butternut squash include cinnamon, cumin, coriander, chile powder, and black pepper. Save the seeds from the squash and roast them as a snack or a topping for soups and salads.

Marrow from 1 roasted marrowbone (optional, see page 99)
1 tablespoon ghee, tallow, or lard
1 cup finely chopped onion
4 garlic cloves, minced
4 cups bone broth of your choice (Chapter 3)
½ cup coconut milk
2 tablespoons raw honey
2 pounds butternut squash, peeled, seeded, and chopped into 1-inch pieces
2 teaspoons curry powder
1 teaspoon Celtic sea salt, plus more to taste
½ teaspoon ground turmeric
¼ teaspoon cayenne pepper
1 tablespoon apple cider vinegar
Freshly ground white pepper

1. In a large stockpot, melt the marrow (if using) and ghee over medium-high heat. Add the onion and garlic and cook until softened, about 10 minutes.

2. Stir in the bone broth, coconut milk, honey, squash, curry powder, salt, turmeric, and cayenne. Bring to a boil, reduce the heat, and simmer for 20 minutes.

3. Working in batches, transfer the soup to a blender and combine until smooth. Be sure to remove the center cover from the lid and hold a towel over the hole to let some steam escape. Return the soup to the pot and stir in the apple cider vinegar. Season with additional salt and white pepper. Serve.

French Onion Soup

Serves 6

PREP
15 minutes

COOK
1 hour 10 minutes

▶ Add cooked chunks of beef to this recipe at the end of cooking for a hearty French onion stew.

French onion soup was originally a peasant dish, prized for its restorative and healing properties. The soup was initially made with various bits and pieces of meat, and the bread was added to thicken it. Today, French onion soup is the ultimate comfort food, and I have updated it for maximum nutrition and flavor with the addition of pâté, making the soup both creamier and richer.

4 cups Beef Bone Broth (page 39), divided
¼ cup Chicken Liver Pâté (page 170) (optional)
Marrow from 2 roasted marrowbones (see page 99)
3 large red onions, thinly sliced
3 large white onions, thinly sliced
2 tablespoons ghee
1 tablespoon raw honey
1 tablespoon apple cider vinegar
1 teaspoon Celtic sea salt, plus more to taste
2 garlic cloves, minced
½ cup dry vermouth
4 cups Chicken Bone Broth (page 41)
3 fresh thyme sprigs
1 bay leaf
Freshly ground black pepper
1½ cups grated Gruyère cheese
12 (1-inch-thick) baguette slices

1. In a saucepan, heat 1 cup of the Beef Bone Broth and add the Chicken Liver Pâté (if using), whisking to combine. Set aside.

2. In a large sauté pan, melt the marrow over medium-high heat. Add the red and white onions and toss to coat. Cook until the onions have softened, 10 to 15 minutes.

3. Increase the heat to medium-high and add the ghee to the pot. Stir the onions frequently until they begin to brown, about 15 more minutes.

4. Sprinkle the honey, apple cider vinegar, and salt over the onions. Add the garlic and stir well. Add the vermouth and stir again, scraping the pot to remove any browned bits.

5. Add the remaining 3 cups Beef Bone Broth and the Chicken Bone Broth, the thyme, and the bay leaf. Bring to a boil, reduce the heat, and simmer for 30 minutes. Season with salt and pepper and remove the bay leaf.

6. Divide the soup among 6 bowls. Top each bowl with ¼ cup cheese and serve with the baguettes.

Detox Soup

Serves 4

PREP
10 minutes

COOK
25 minutes

▶ Leeks can be extremely dirty in between the layers of their flesh. To thoroughly wash leeks, cut off the ends, slice the entire root in half lengthwise, and soak the leeks in fresh water, agitating the leeks to remove as much dirt as possible. Change the water several times during the process until it remains clear.

Whether or not you are on a detox diet program, you will enjoy this simple and nourishing soup. I designed it to be immune boosting and soothing to your system, and it's full of clean, fresh ingredients. Thanks to the mushrooms, kale, and spinach, it has a savory flavor profile, while a bit of pâté adds body and seasoning to the soup—for a richer and thicker texture, just add a touch more.

1 tablespoon tallow
Marrow from 1 roasted marrowbone (optional, page 99)
1 cup thinly sliced fennel
½ cup thinly sliced leek
1 teaspoon grated fresh ginger
4 cups bone broth of your choice (Chapter 3)
2 tablespoons Chicken Liver Pâté (page 170, optional)
1 cup maitake mushrooms
1 cup cooked lentils
4 celery stalks, thinly sliced
1 cup chopped kale
1 cup chopped spinach

1. In a large stockpot, heat the tallow. Add the marrow (if using) and allow it to melt.

2. Add the fennel, leek, and ginger and cook until the vegetables become soft.

3. Pour in the bone broth and bring the soup to a boil. Reduce the heat to a simmer and add the Chicken Liver Pâté (if using), stirring until well incorporated.

4. Add the mushrooms and lentils and continue to simmer for 15 more minutes.

5. Remove the pot from the heat and add the celery, kale, and spinach. Stir well and serve immediately.

Summer Gazpacho

Serves 6

PREP

25 minutes,
plus 25 minutes to chill

▶ For a spicy gazpacho,
de-seed and chop one
jalapeño and add it to
the vegetables before
blending.

A Spanish gem, gazpacho is easy to make and refreshing. It requires no cooking, so this recipe is a perfect vessel for bone broth on a warm summer's day. I recommend that you use a batch of broth that didn't gel for the best texture. Enjoy with a crusty baguette and chilled glass of white wine.

5 tomatoes, roughly diced

1 red onion, roughly diced

1 cucumber, roughly diced

3 celery stalks, chopped

2 tablespoons chopped parsley

1 clove garlic, minced

2 cups bone broth of your choice, non-gelled, if desired

¼ cup apple cider vinegar

1 tablespoon aged balsamic vinegar

¼ cup olive oil

1 tablespoon lemon juice

2 tablespoons dried basil

3 tablespoons raw cane sugar (or more if needed to balance acid levels)

1 teaspoon Celtic sea salt

1 teaspoon freshly ground pepper

4 radishes, finely chopped, for garnish

1. Combine the tomatoes, onion, cucumber, celery, parsley, and garlic in a large mixing bowl. Pulse the vegetables with an immersion blender.

2. Slowly add the bone broth, apple cider vinegar, balsamic vinegar, olive oil, and lemon juice, pulsing occasionally, until the vegetables have combined and you have reached your desired consistency (gazpacho can be either chunky or smooth). Add the dried basil, sugar, salt, and pepper and stir to combine.

3. Allow the gazpacho to chill in your refrigerator for at least 25 minutes before serving. Season to taste. Garnish with the chopped radish.

Garlic and Mushroom Soup

Serves 6

PREP
15 minutes

COOK
20 minutes

▶ For an extra dose of vitamin C, add a squeeze of lemon juice to this soup right before serving.

This simple soup is perfect if you're feeling under the weather or need something comforting to sip on. The effortless flavor gives you the freedom of a blank slate, so you can add seasonal vegetables or any protein you might be craving and make it different every time. It keeps for one week in the refrigerator or six months in the freezer, and can be very handy to keep on hand when you need a quick meal base.

2 tablespoons tallow
10–15 cloves garlic (about one head), peeled and thinly sliced
1 teaspoon dried thyme or 2 teaspoons fresh thyme
1 quart bone broth of your choice (see Chapter 3)
½ teaspoon Celtic sea salt
½ teaspoon pepper
1 cup white mushrooms, thinly sliced
¼ cup thinly sliced chives for garnish

1. Melt the tallow in a deep saucepan on low heat. Add the garlic slices and gently stir them on a low heat until they become soft and translucent, about 3–5 minutes. Be careful not to burn or scorch the garlic.

2. Add the thyme and gently stir until it becomes fragrant, about 3–5 minutes. Add the broth, salt, and pepper and allow all the ingredients to simmer on a low heat for 20 minutes.

3. Add the mushrooms. Garnish each bowl with a sprinkling of chives and serve piping hot.

Tom Kha Soup

Serves 6

PREP
10 minutes

COOK
40 minutes

Tom kha, or Thai coconut soup, has the same medicinal reputation in Thailand as does our American chicken soup. This is the soup I crave when I am sick. It's spicy and sweet, with warm soothing coconut milk and a mélange of citrus flavors. First documented in the sixteenth century, lemongrass and ginger have long been known to soothe upset tummies.

Marrow from 1 roasted marrowbone (optional, see page 99)

6 cups bone broth of your choice (Chapter 3)

2 lemongrass stalks, tough outer leaves removed, stalks cut into 4-inch pieces

1 (2-inch) piece ginger, peeled

1 tablespoon grated lime zest

2 tablespoons freshly squeezed lime juice

3 tablespoons apple cider vinegar, divided

1 cup sliced maitake or oyster mushroom caps

1 head bok choy, thinly sliced

2 carrots, thinly sliced on an angle

1 cup coconut milk

2 tablespoons fish sauce

1 teaspoon raw honey

1. In a large saucepan, melt the marrow (if using) over medium-high heat. Add the broth, lemongrass, ginger, lime zest, lime juice, and 2 tablespoons of the apple cider vinegar. Stir to combine.

2. Bring the mixture to a boil, reduce the heat to a simmer, and cook for 15 minutes. Strain the broth into a large bowl and discard the solids.

3. Return the broth to the pan and add the mushrooms, bok choy, and carrots. Cook for 25 minutes.

4. Remove the pot from the heat, stir in the coconut milk, fish sauce, honey, and remaining 1 tablespoon of apple cider vinegar. Serve.

Pregnancy Soup

Serves 4

PREP
5 minutes

COOK
25 minutes (plus 5 to 10 minutes steeping time)

▶ This is also a great post-pregnancy soup to supply nourishment to the body after childbirth, especially if you're breastfeeding.

Whether you're ravenously eating for two or feeling too queasy for anything solid, pregnancy is an ideal time for soothing soups and sips. This is a very adaptable soup. I have also included optional additions to this soup for varying pregnancy issues—add the ingredients that your body craves. Always consult your doctor before consuming herbs and small amounts of liver during pregnancy.

FOR THE SOUP BASE
Marrow from 1 roasted marrowbone (see page 99)
1 medium fennel bulb, cored and thinly sliced
1 teaspoon grated fresh ginger
4 cups bone broth of your choice (Chapter 3)

FOR THE NUTRIENT-FOCUSED ADDITIONS
Vitamin-Building: add a handful of grated carrots, grated beets, and/or grated zucchini
Iron-Building: add a handful of spinach and/or dried nettles
Stomach-Soothing: add 2 fresh muddled peppermint sprigs or 2 or 3 drops peppermint oil
Labor-Inducing: add watercress, red cabbage, chili oil, and balsamic vinegar

TO MAKE THE SOUP BASE

1. In a large stockpot, melt the marrow. Add the fennel and ginger and cook until softened, about 5 minutes.

2. Add the bone broth and bring to a boil. Reduce the heat, and simmer on low heat for 15 minutes. Remove from heat.

TO MAKE THE NUTRIENT-FOCUSED ADDITIONS

1. Add the desired additions to the soup.

2. Cover and allow to steep for 5 to 10 minutes. Serve.

Superfood Soup

Serves 4

PREP
20 minutes

COOK
1 hour 10 minutes

▶ This can easily be made into a superfood salad. Omit the hot broth, cooked rice, and lentils, and replace with dressing for a vegetable-based salad.

I developed this soup for a client who was looking for quick, healthy lunches and dinners. Keep batches of it in the freezer and you will always be ready when hunger strikes. It's chock-full of the most delicious superfoods to keep you feeling your best, but if you have other favorite vegetables or ingredients you'd like to include, feel free to use them in this versatile soup. The addition of salmon fillets adds a nice dose of protein and omega-3 fatty acids.

1 teaspoon tallow
Marrow from 2 roasted marrowbones (optional, see page 99)
1 large fennel bulb, cored and thinly sliced
1 cup shiitake mushrooms
1 garlic clove, minced
1 teaspoon grated fresh ginger
5 cups bone broth of your choice (Chapter 3)
2 cups cooked sprouted brown rice (see page 93)
1 cup cooked lentils
1 cup spinach
2 cups thinly sliced bok choy
4 baked salmon fillets
1 avocado, sliced, for garnish

1. In a large pot, heat the tallow and marrow (if using) until they are liquefied.

2. Add the fennel and cook until it begins to soften. Add the shiitake mushrooms and cook for another 3 minutes.

3. Add the garlic and ginger, and cook, stirring continuously, for 2 minutes.

4. Add the broth and bring to a boil; reduce the heat and simmer for 1 hour.

5. To serve, spoon ½ cup brown rice into each bowl. Top with ¼ cup lentils, ¼ cup spinach, and ½ cup bok choy.

6. Pour 1¼ cups of broth over each bowl. Cover and let rest for 5 minutes. Top each bowl with a piece of salmon, garnish with avocado, and serve.

Shrimp Soup for the Soul

Serves 2

PREP
15 minutes

COOK
35 minutes

Creamy puréed celery root serves as the base of this soup, providing a mild backdrop for the delicious shrimp, sliced chard, and spicy chili oil. Make this soup as thick or thin as you like by adding more or less bone broth. If you prefer, you can substitute another type of shellfish or fish in place of the shrimp, such as seared scallops or poached salmon.

1 tablespoon ghee, tallow, or lard
1 fennel bulb, cored and thinly sliced
1 white onion, halved and sliced
2 garlic cloves, minced
6 jumbo shrimp, peeled, deveined, and butterflied
2 cups Fish Bone Broth (page 56) or Shellfish Broth (page 58)
2 cups Whipped Celery Root (page 154)
¼ cup dry white wine
2 teaspoons apple cider vinegar
1 teaspoon Celtic sea salt
1 teaspoon freshly ground white pepper
½ cup thinly sliced chard leaves
Chili oil, for garnish

1. In a large saucepan, melt the ghee over medium-high heat. Add the fennel and onion and cook until soft and translucent, stirring frequently.

2. Add the garlic and shrimp to the pan and cook until the shrimp are pink and fully cooked. Remove the shrimp with a slotted spoon and set aside.

3. Add the bone broth, Whipped Celery Root, and white wine to the pot. Bring to a boil, reduce the heat, and simmer for 15 minutes.

4. Remove the soup from the heat and add the apple cider vinegar, salt, and pepper. Ladle the soup into two bowls. Top each bowl with half of the shrimp and chard, drizzle with chili oil, and serve.

Pho with Zoodles

Serves 6 to 8

PREP
20 minutes

COOK
1 hour 10 minutes

▶ If you like, you can sub in other cooked meats or seafood for this dish. Use the broth of your desired meat for extra flavor.

Pho is thought to have been introduced to Vietnam during the French occupation in the late nineteenth century. The term "pho" likely comes from the French dish pot-au-feu, *a marrow-rich beef stew that literally translates to "pot on fire." As Vietnamese migrated to the United States, the dish became very popular here as well. I have replaced traditional noodles with "zoodles" (spiral-sliced zucchini) for a fun, Paleo-friendly substitution.*

1 tablespoon tallow
Marrow from 2 roasted marrowbones (optional, see page 99)
1 large fennel bulb, cored and thinly sliced
1 (3-inch) piece ginger, thinly sliced on an angle
1 large white onion, cut in half and charred
3 star anise pods
1 cinnamon stick
4 cloves
1 teaspoon coriander seeds
8 cups bone broth of your choice (Chapter 3)
6 to 8 medium zucchini, spiralized or julienned
1 pound shredded chicken
½ cup thinly sliced scallions
3 to 5 jalapeños, seeded if desired and thinly sliced on an angle
3 limes, quartered
Hoisin sauce, for serving
Sambal sauce, for serving

1. In a large stockpot, heat the tallow over medium-high heat. Add the marrow (if using) and stir to combine with the tallow.

2. Add the fennel to the pot and cook, stirring often, until it begins to soften.

3. Stir in the ginger, onion, star anise, cinnamon stick, cloves, and coriander seeds and cook for 3 minutes.

4. Add the broth to the pot and bring to a boil. Reduce the heat and simmer for 1 hour, stirring occasionally. ▶

Pho with Zoodles continued

5. Remove the pot from the heat and add the zoodles. Cover and allow to stand for 5 minutes.

6. Divide the zoodles between 6 to 8 bowls and ladle the stock into the bowls to fill.

7. Arrange the shredded chicken on a large serving plate; on another plate, arrange the scallions, jalapeños, and limes.

8. Invite each diner to add the shredded chicken to the hot broth and garnish with the other items as desired. Add hoisin and sambal sauce according to taste.

Steamed Clams in Bone Broth and Cider

Serves 4

PREP
20 minutes

COOK
20 minutes

▶ This savory seafood preparation does not need to be limited to clams. Use the same seasonings to make steamed mussels or a mixed seafood dish.

Recently I taught a large cooking class for a local San Diego charity, Collaboration Kitchen. Inspired by the northern region of France, where apples and cream are prevalent, I created this sweet and spicy dish. The clams, when combined with cider and grated apples, possess an appetizing sweetness, while jalapeños add a spicy counterpoint. The dish was a hit that night in the class and will definitely be a crowd pleaser with your friends and family.

1 large Fuji apple, peeled, cored, and grated
1 large jalapeño, seeded and grated, divided
Grated zest of 3 limes, divided
1 bunch parsley, minced
1½ teaspoons olive oil
6 garlic cloves, minced
2 medium shallots, minced
½ cup bone broth of your choice (Chapter 3)
½ cup hard cider
½ cup crème fraîche (optional)
3 pounds clams
1 lime

1. Combine the apple, half of the jalapeño, and half of the lime zest in a bowl and set aside.

2. Combine the parsley and the remaining jalapeño and lime zest in another bowl and set aside.

3. In a medium pot, heat the olive oil over medium-high heat. Add the garlic and shallots and cook until they are translucent, stirring constantly.

4. Add the bone broth, cider, and crème fraîche (if using). Whisk until the crème fraîche is well incorporated into the liquid. ▶

Steamed Clams
in Bone Broth and Cider continued

5. Add the clams and the reserved apple, jalapeño, and lime zest mixture from step 1. Cover and cook until all the clams open, 20 to 25 minutes.

6. Remove the pot from the heat, and squeeze the lime juice over the clams. Garnish with the parsley, jalapeño, and lime zest mixture from step 2 and serve.

Cioppino

Serves 4 to 6

PREP
20 minutes

COOK
1 hour 15 minutes

▶ Cioppino is a filling soup perfect for a cold winter night. To make it an even heartier meal, serve warm, crusty bread alongside for dipping.

This one-pot dish is a showstopper for your dinner table. Cioppino features garlic, onions, peppers, and tomatoes as a juicy backdrop for a mixture of fresh seafood and fish. While Dungeness crab is most traditional for this dish, use whatever seafood is freshest at your fish market. I suggest using a combination of fish stock and shellfish broth in this recipe to deepen the layers of flavor.

3 tablespoons ghee, tallow, or lard

1 medium onion, chopped

1 celery stalk, sliced

4 garlic cloves, sliced

4 cups chopped fresh tomatoes, lightly salted and resting in juices for 20 minutes

½ cup sliced roasted red peppers

1 teaspoon dried thyme

1 teaspoon dried oregano

1 teaspoon red pepper flakes

2 cups Fish Bone Broth (page 56)

½ cup dry white wine

1 cup Shellfish Broth (page 58)

½ pound scallops

1 pound firm white fish

1 pound medium shrimp, peeled and deveined

24 medium clams

1 tablespoon freshly squeezed lemon juice

1 tablespoon apple cider vinegar

1 teaspoon Celtic sea salt

½ teaspoon freshly ground black pepper

¼ cup chopped fresh parsley, for garnish

1. In a stockpot, heat the ghee over medium-high heat.

2. Add the onion, celery, and garlic and cook until the vegetables become very tender and begin to brown, about 15 minutes. ▶

Cioppino continued

3. Stir in the tomatoes and their juices. Add the roasted peppers, thyme, oregano, and red pepper flakes. Pour in the Fish Bone Broth and wine and bring to a simmer. Partially cover the pot and cook for 45 minutes.

4. Pour in the Shellfish Broth and cook for another 5 minutes.

5. Add the scallops and white fish and cook until they become firm and opaque, about 5 minutes.

6. Add the shrimp and clams and continue to cook until the shrimp turn pink and the clams open, 7 to 10 more minutes.

7. Mix in the lemon juice and the apple cider vinegar. Stir in the salt and pepper. Serve in bowls, garnished with parsley.

Master Tonic Soup

Serves 4

PREP
15 minutes

COOK
1 hour

▶ You can freeze this soup in single servings to pull out and reheat when someone in your home is feeling under the weather. Reheat the serving in a small saucepan, and then add the Master Tonic vegetables and liquid as directed.

Once you have produced a batch of Master Tonic (page 64), you'll be able to use it in dozens of ways. This soup is meant to be restorative and will have you feeling better in no time. With this soup in your repertoire, you'll soon be on your way to recovery!

1½ teaspoons tallow or lard
Marrow from 2 roasted marrowbones (optional, see page 99)
1 large white onion, cut in half and thinly sliced
1 large fennel bulb, cored and thinly sliced
3 large carrots, cut into bite-size chunks
2 celery stalks, thinly sliced
3 thyme sprigs, tied into a bundle
2½ cups shredded cooked chicken
4 cups Chicken Bone Broth (page 41)
1 teaspoon Celtic sea salt
4 tablespoons Master Tonic vegetable pieces (see page 64), divided
4 tablespoons Master Tonic liquid (see page 64), divided

1. In a large stockpot, heat the tallow over medium-high heat until it melts. Add the marrow (if using) and heat until it melts.

2. Add the onion, fennel, carrots, celery, and thyme and cook until the vegetables just begin to soften.

3. Stir in the chicken meat and broth. Bring the broth to a boil, reduce the heat to a simmer, and cook for 45 minutes.

4. Remove the pot from the heat and add the salt.

5. Ladle the soup into four bowls and add 1 tablespoon each of Master Tonic vegetables and liquid to each bowl. Serve.

Mason Jar Lentil Chicken Curry

Serves 1

PREP
10 minutes

COOK
5 minutes (plus
10 minutes resting
time)

▶ Mason jar soups are
perfect for leftovers!
Just layer any leftover
meats, beans, and
vegetables into a jar,
leaving room for the
added broth, and you
have a meal to go in
minutes.

Skip the peanut butter and jelly sandwich in your lunch box. Mason jar soups are fun to prepare and eat and are infinitely adaptable—perfect for either school or work. All you need to do is fill a mason jar with your favorite ingredients and you've got a quick lunch to go. This soup contains a good deal of fiber and protein, and its exotic, warming flavors will delight your taste buds.

2 teaspoons curry powder
1 teaspoon ground turmeric
¼ cup coconut milk
¼ cup cooked lentils
¼ cup shredded cooked chicken
¼ cup grated zucchini
¼ cup chopped green beans
¾ cup bone broth of your choice (Chapter 3)

1. In a 12-ounce mason jar, whisk together the curry powder, turmeric, and coconut milk.

2. Making layers in the jar, first add the lentils, followed by the chicken, the zucchini, and then the green beans. Cover and refrigerate until ready to serve.

3. When ready to serve, bring the bone broth to a simmer in a small saucepan over medium-high heat. Pour the broth into the jar, cover, and let stand for 10 minutes.

Creamy Greek Lemon Soup (Avgolemono)

Serves 4

PREP
10 minutes

COOK
40 minutes

▶ If you prefer a lighter lemon flavor, cut the lemon juice to just 2 tablespoons. For this recipe, be sure to use freshly squeezed lemon juice, which has a much brighter and stronger flavor than bottled varieties.

The name of this soup literally translates to "egg lemon" and was thought to be brought to Greece by Sephardic Jews from elsewhere in Europe. For this soup I prefer lamb broth, a favorite in Greek cuisine, but you can sub-stitute chicken broth. I have omitted the traditional potatoes and added fennel, turnips, and onion instead for a more flavorful and hearty meal.

2 tablespoons tallow
2 large fennel bulbs, cored and thinly sliced
2 large carrots, diced
1 cup diced turnip
4 cups Lamb Bone Broth (page 46)
1 cup cooked white rice
2 large egg yolks
¼ cup freshly squeezed lemon juice
1½ pounds shredded cooked lamb or chicken
½ cup chopped fresh dill

1. In a large stockpot, melt the tallow over medium-high heat.

2. Add the fennel, carrots, and turnip and sauté until the fennel becomes soft.

3. Add the broth and bring to a simmer.

4. Using a ladle, transfer 1½ cups hot broth to a blender. Add the rice, egg yolks, and lemon juice and purée until smooth. Be sure to remove the center cover from the lid and hold a towel over the hole to allow steam to escape.

5. Add the meat to the stockpot and simmer until the vegetables are fork-tender, about 15 minutes.

6. Add the rice and egg yolk purée to the stockpot and simmer until thickened, about another 10 minutes. Garnish with the dill and serve.

Duck Ramen

Serves 4

PREP
10 minutes

COOK
20 minutes

Everyone loves ramen, and duck ramen is a particularly rich and satisfying dish, perfect for a cold night. I like to throw ramen bar dinner parties. Line up bowls of various toppings—such as hard-boiled eggs, scallions, cilantro, grated carrots, bok choy, shiitake mushrooms, and jalapeños— and serve each guest a bowl of plain broth and noodles to customize to their taste.

1 tablespoon tallow
Marrow from 1 roasted marrowbone (optional, see page 99)
6 garlic cloves, minced
1 tablespoon grated fresh ginger
6 cups Duck Bone Broth (page 44)
1 tablespoon liquid aminos
3 packages instant ramen noodles, seasoning packets discarded
2 cups shredded cooked duck
2 eggs, hardboiled and cut in half
2 tablespoons thinly sliced scallions
1 cup of crisped duck skin, chopped, for garnish (optional)

1. In a large stockpot, heat the tallow and marrow (if using) over medium-high heat to liquefy.

2. Add the garlic and ginger and cook until they become aromatic, about 30 seconds.

3. Add the Duck Bone Broth and liquid aminos, stirring to combine. Bring to a boil and add the noodles, stirring to loosen and separate them. Reduce the heat to a simmer and cook the noodles for 2 minutes.

4. Divide the noodles and vegetables evenly among 4 bowls. Divide the duck meat among the bowls. Add an egg half to each bowl. Cover the noodles with the broth, garnish with the scallions and crispy duck skin (if using), and serve.

Posole

PREP
15 minutes

COOK
6 hours in a slow cooker, plus 1 hour and 10 minutes on the stove top

Posole is one of my favorite soups to enjoy on a winter's day. Dating back to pre-Hispanic times, this hearty soup has been recorded as part of indigenous celebrations. Today it is served in different variations in many regions of Mexico. In Guerrero they add green tomatoes and in Michoacán, a region famous for its carnitas, they add crispy pork skin known as chicharrón. *Don't forget the avocado and lime garnishes.*

FOR THE PORK

1 tablespoon ground cumin

1 teaspoon ground turmeric

1 teaspoon Celtic sea salt

1 (2-pound) pork shoulder

2 tablespoons lard

½ cup smoked sausage, finely chopped

1 cup Pork Bone Broth (page 48)

FOR THE POSOLE

2 tablespoons lard

½ red onion, chopped

5 garlic cloves, minced

2 ripe tomatoes, diced

6 cups Pork Bone Broth (page 48)

1 (28-ounce) can hominy

2 tablespoons ground cumin

1 tablespoon dried Mexican oregano

1 tablespoon ground turmeric

3 tablespoons apple cider vinegar

Celtic sea salt

Freshly ground black pepper

Corn tortillas, for serving

Chopped fresh cilantro, for garnish

Lime wedges, for garnish

Avocado slices, for garnish

TO MAKE THE PORK SHOULDER

1. In a small bowl, combine the cumin, turmeric, and salt. Rub this spice mix all over the pork.

2. Heat the lard in a large cast-iron pan and sear the pork shoulder on all sides. Transfer the pork shoulder to a slow cooker. Add the sausage to the pan and cook for 5 minutes, then transfer to the slow cooker. Add the Pork Bone Broth to the pan and use a wooden spoon to loosen any extra bits of meat, and then pour the broth into the slow cooker.

3. Cover and cook on high for 6 hours. Remove the pork from the slow cooker, reserving the broth. Shred the pork with two forks and set aside.

TO MAKE THE POSOLE

1. In a large pot, heat the lard over medium-low heat.

2. Add the red onion and sauté until translucent, about 5 minutes.

3. Add the garlic and cook, stirring often, until soft and fragrant, about 2 minutes.

4. Add the diced tomatoes and stir until softened, about 2 minutes.

5. Stir in the broth, followed by the hominy, cumin, oregano, and turmeric. Stir well to combine. Cover and simmer, stirring occasionally, for 30 minutes.

6. Add the shredded pork to the pot. Simmer, uncovered, until the flavors begin to meld, about 30 minutes.

7. Add the apple cider vinegar and season with salt and pepper as desired. Serve with tortillas and garnish with chopped cilantro, lime wedges, and avocado slices.

Autumnal Pork Stew

Serves 8 to 10

PREP
15 minutes

COOK
Slow Cooker:
4 hours on high or
8 hours on low

▶ This autumnal stew gets better the longer it sits. For an extra-flavorful stew, prepare it a day before serving.

This is my favorite recipe in this book. I created it on a whim, adding a variety of unexpected ingredients including orange marmalade, brandy, and smoked sausage. When cooked in a slow cooker, the result is tender, smoky pork in a rich broth perfumed by notes of citrus and spice. The sweet squash and apple complement the savory meat and broth, while the brandy adds a beautiful finish, heightening all the aromatic elements.

1 teaspoon tallow
1 (1½-pound) pork shoulder, cubed
½ cup finely chopped smoked pork sausage
4 cups diced butternut squash
1 large white onion, chopped
1 small fennel bulb, cored and thinly sliced
½ Fuji apple, peeled, cored and finely chopped
3½ cups bone broth of your choice (Chapter 3)
¼ cup brandy
3 tablespoons orange marmalade
3 sage sprigs, tied into a bundle
1½ teaspoons Celtic sea salt
2 tablespoons apple cider vinegar

1. In a large stockpot, heat the tallow over medium-high heat. Add the pork cubes and cook until well browned, stirring frequently. Transfer to a slow cooker using a slotted spoon.

2. Add the sausage to the pot and brown well. Transfer to the slow cooker.

3. Add the butternut squash, onion, fennel, apple, bone broth, brandy, orange marmalade, and sage to the slow cooker. Cover and cook on high for 4 hours or on low for 8 hours.

4. Stir in the salt and apple cider vinegar. Serve.

Boeuf Bourguignon

Serves 6

PREP
10 minutes

COOK
3 hours

▶ You can cook this in a slow cooker on the low setting for 6 hours. Follow steps 1 through 4 in a pan, and then transfer to the slow cooker.

French food has a way of warming my soul, and this stew is no exception. I've adapted this recipe from early twentieth-century France, using elements such as tallow and marrow from bones, but have otherwise kept the recipe as close to the original as I can. It's best made a few days before serving so the flavors can fully develop.

¼ cup tallow
2 pounds stew beef, cubed
Marrow from 3 roasted marrowbones (see page 99)
4 white onions, thinly sliced
1 cup sliced shiitake mushrooms
2 tablespoons flour (optional)
1 cup dry red wine
6 bacon slices, cooked, drained, and chopped
6 medium carrots, cut into bite-size pieces
2 garlic cloves, minced
1 bouquet garni
2 tablespoons balsamic vinegar
2 to 4 cups bone broth of your choice (Chapter 3)

1. In a Dutch oven, heat the tallow over high heat. Add the beef cubes and cook until browned on all sides. Use a slotted spoon to transfer the beef to a plate and set aside.

2. Add the marrow to the pot and heat until melted. Add the onions and mushrooms and cook until beginning to soften, 6 to 8 minutes.

3. Sprinkle the flour (if using) into the pot and stir well with the mushrooms and onions. Continue cooking, stirring frequently, for 5 minutes.

4. Add the red wine to deglaze the pot, scraping the bottom of the pot to remove any browned pieces.

5. Return the beef to the pot. Add the bacon, carrots, garlic, bouquet garni, and balsamic vinegar. Add enough bone broth to cover. Bring to a boil and then lower the heat to a simmer. Cover the pot and cook until the meat is fork-tender, stirring occasionally, about 2½ hours. Remove the bouquet garni and serve.

CHAPTER 8

FROM THE GARDEN

I*n my quest to live a traditional foods lifestyle, I have found meat to be more and more a rarity at my table. My dinner plates tend to be filled with two or three vegetables and, on a special occasion, a piece of meat. It's a great rule of thumb to live by. This chapter includes some of my favorite veggie recipes, all of which are enhanced by the comforting flavors of bone broth. Most are simple in their preparation and can please any crowd.*

Quick-Seared Veggies

Serves 4

PREP
5 minutes

COOK
10 minutes

▶ These veggies are excellent cold—and a great replacement snack for a bag of chips.

This is my favorite way to make vegetables, and I think you'll love it, too. It's quick and easy and you can make enough at once to snack on all week. By searing the vegetables, you develop a deeper intensity of their intrinsic character, while retaining the health benefits of their raw state. Adding the garlic at the end provides an excellent pop of flavor.

1 tablespoon tallow
1 head broccoli, stem peeled, cut lengthwise into 8 long stalks
1 bunch small to medium carrots, greens trimmed,
   tops intact, cut in half lengthwise
¼ cup bone broth of your choice (Chapter 3)
6 garlic cloves, minced
1 teaspoon olive oil
½ teaspoon Celtic sea salt

1. In a large cast-iron pan, melt the tallow over medium-high heat.

2. Add the broccoli and carrots and sear on each side, 3 to 5 minutes.

3. Add the bone broth to the pan and simmer until it completely evaporates.

4. Remove the pan from the heat, add the garlic, and stir to incorporate.

5. Drizzle with the olive oil, sprinkle on the salt, and serve.

Broccoli "Rice" with Currants

Serves 4

PREP
5 minutes

COOK
10 minutes

► Grate a good cheese over this, like Parmesan or a dry sheep's cheese, to increase its savory appeal.

Finely chopped broccoli or cauliflower produces a fine stand-in for rice. This simple recipe makes a great side dish that is both healthier and tastier than plain white or even brown rice—and takes very little time and effort to prepare. Currants add a pleasant sweetness to the dish.

1 tablespoon ghee, tallow, or lard
1 small red onion, finely chopped
1 garlic clove, minced
1 head broccoli, florets removed and finely chopped
½ cup bone broth of your choice (Chapter 3)
¾ cup currants
1 teaspoon olive oil
½ teaspoon Celtic sea salt

1. In a large skillet, melt the ghee over medium-high heat. Add the onion and garlic and cook, stirring occasionally, until softened and translucent.

2. Add the broccoli and stir to combine. Increase the heat to high and add the bone broth to the skillet. Simmer, uncovered, until the bone broth evaporates.

3. Toss in the currants, drizzle with the olive oil, and season with the salt. Serve.

Strawberry-Spiced Glazed Carrots

Serves 4

PREP
5 minutes

COOK
40 minutes

▶ You can use this recipe with other root vegetables—like turnips or beets—with great results.

Carrots and strawberries might sound like an unusual combination, but it's actually quite delightful. A long roast brings out the sweetness in the carrots, while the spiciness of the strawberry-jalapeño jam adds a wonderful accent. Caramelizing the carrots produces a lacquered finish and a beautiful color. Carrots lose flavor over time, so use the freshest, tastiest carrots you can find, and the dish will be truly special. This recipe pairs wonderfully with Chicken or Rabbit Mole (page 165) and the Zucchini Fritters (page 155).

½ cup bone broth of your choice (Chapter 3)
2 tablespoons strawberry-jalapeño jam
1 teaspoon balsamic vinegar
1½ teaspoons tallow, melted
2 bunches carrots, greens trimmed, tops intact

1. Preheat the oven to 375°F.

2. In a small saucepan, whisk together the bone broth, jam, and vinegar over medium heat.

3. Line a small baking dish with aluminum foil; the dish should be small enough that the carrots fit snugly. Put the melted tallow in the dish, and then add the carrots so they become coated in tallow. Pour the broth mixture over the carrots.

4. Bake the carrots for 25 minutes. Change the oven setting to broil, and broil the carrots until the sauce thickens and begins to caramelize, about 10 more minutes. Serve.

Cauliflower Steaks with Walnut Chimichurri

Serves 4

PREP

20 minutes (plus 1 hour resting time)

COOK

15 minutes

▶ This walnut chimichurri is an excellent condiment to have on hand. It complements any type of meat, can be stirred into soups and stews, and is an excellent appetizer addition to any table. It can be made up to 1 day before serving and refrigerated until ready for use.

Cauliflower stands in nicely for an actual steak, and you can top it with almost anything. In this case I've combined rich walnuts with the herbal and acidic chimichurri, a green sauce originally from Argentina and still popular today throughout Latin America. Chimichurri is typically served with grilled meat; though the sauce is paired here with a vegetable. Cooking the cauliflower in beef tallow gives it a bit of a beefy aroma.

⅔ cup apple cider vinegar
½ cup olive oil
1 tablespoon raw honey
1 tablespoon preserved lemon juice
1 tablespoon finely chopped preserved lemon rind
1 teaspoon ground turmeric
1 teaspoon Celtic sea salt
1 teaspoon cayenne pepper
1 cup raw walnuts, lightly toasted and finely chopped
8 garlic cloves, minced
1 cup minced fresh parsley
½ cup minced fresh cilantro
1 teaspoon minced fresh rosemary
1 tablespoon tallow
1 large head cauliflower, stem and leaves removed,
    cut lengthwise into 4 (¾-inch-thick) "steaks"
½ cup bone broth of your choice (Chapter 3)

1. In a medium bowl, whisk together the apple cider vinegar, olive oil, honey, preserved lemon juice, preserved lemon rind, turmeric, salt, and cayenne.

2. Add the walnuts, garlic, parsley, cilantro, and rosemary to the bowl. Toss to coat entirely. Allow to sit at room temperature for 1 hour before serving or refrigerating. ▶

Cauliflower Steaks with
Walnut Chimichurri continued

3. In a large cast-iron pan, heat the tallow over medium-high heat.

4. Add 2 cauliflower steaks to the pan, searing on each side until golden brown, about 3 minutes per side.

5. Add ¼ cup bone broth to the pan and simmer, uncovered, until the liquid has completely evaporated. Transfer the steaks to a plate. Repeat the cooking process with the remaining cauliflower steaks and bone broth.

6. To serve, put each cauliflower steak on a plate and serve with the walnut chimichurri.

Mixed Mushroom Larb

Serves 4

PREP
10 minutes

COOK
20 minutes

This is a vegetable-focused version of one of my favorite dishes, the spicy meat salad known in Laos and Thailand as larb. The sautéed mushrooms lend a healthy, meaty texture, along with a sweet, bright flavor thanks to the combination of ginger, garlic, coconut, and fresh mint. You can make this ahead of time to allow the flavors to meld, and serve at your convenience for a quick lunch or no-hassle dinner.

1 tablespoon ghee, tallow, or lard
½ cup diced white onion
1 garlic clove, minced
1 teaspoon grated fresh ginger
3 cups chopped mixed mushrooms
¾ cup Duck Bone Broth (page 44) or Beef Bone Broth (page 39)
1 cup chopped broccoli
½ cup diced red onion
½ cup unsweetened shredded coconut
2 tablespoons chopped fresh mint
¼ cup Spicy Asian Dressing or Marinade (page 105)
4 large lettuce leaves

1. In a large skillet, heat the ghee over medium-high heat. Add the white onion, garlic, and ginger and cook until the onion becomes soft and translucent, about 10 minutes.

2. Add the mushrooms to the pan, stirring to combine. Add the bone broth and simmer until the broth is completely evaporated, about 5 minutes.

3. Stir in the broccoli, red onion, coconut, and mint and cook for another 5 minutes.

4. Remove the pan from the heat, stir in the dressing, and serve in lettuce cups.

Ratatouille

PREP
15 minutes

COOK
35 minutes

▶ Serve this with a
fresh farmer's cheese
garnished with herbs
or a ball of burrata.
For the most flavor,
make the ratatouille
1 to 2 days in advance
of serving to give the
flavors plenty of time
to meld.

*Ratatouille was created by peasant farmers in France, in and around the
area of Nice. The term* ratatouille *comes from the French word,* touiller,
*which means "to toss." The addition of the marrow, ghee, and bone broth
gives this bright and sunny dish a rich texture. Use vegetables from your
garden or those you gather from your local farmers' market on a warm
summer day.*

Marrow from 2 roasted marrowbones (see page 99) or 1 tablespoon ghee
1 onion, sliced
3 garlic cloves, minced
3 tablespoons ghee, tallow, or lard
1 pound eggplant, diced
1 large fennel bulb, cored and thinly sliced
1 medium zucchini, diced
1 red bell pepper, diced
1 pound tomatoes, diced
½ cup bone broth of your choice (Chapter 3)
1 teaspoon Celtic sea salt
½ teaspoon freshly ground black pepper
¼ teaspoon dried oregano
¼ teaspoon dried thyme
⅛ teaspoon ground coriander
½ cup shredded fresh basil

1. In a large pan, melt the marrow or ghee over medium heat. Add the
onion and garlic and cook, stirring often, until the onion is softened and
translucent, about 10 minutes.

2. Add the ghee to the pan. Add the eggplant and fennel and cook,
stirring occasionally, until the eggplant is softened, about 8 minutes.

3. Stir in the zucchini and the bell pepper and cook, stirring
occasionally, until soft, about 10 minutes.

4. Add the tomatoes and bone broth and simmer, stirring occasionally,
until the vegetables are tender, about 7 minutes.

5. Stir in the salt, pepper, oregano, thyme, and coriander. Remove the
pan from the heat, stir in the basil, and serve.

Whipped Celery Root

Serves 4 to 6

PREP
10 minutes

COOK
30 minutes

▶ If your resulting purée is too liquidy, transfer it to a saucepan and allow it to reduce over medium-high heat until you reach the desired consistency.

Available year-round, celery root (also known as celeriac) tastes like a cross between celery and parsley. With its snowy white flesh, it can be cooked like any other root vegetable but can also be served raw in salads. It easily replaces potatoes in any dish. If you can't find celery root in your local grocery store, substitute 1 head cauliflower and 2 cups chopped celery.

2 pounds celery root
1 medium onion, chopped
3 garlic cloves, peeled
2 cups bone broth of your choice (Chapter 3)
½ cup pastured butter, ghee, tallow, or lard
¼ cup coconut milk

1. Remove the green tops from each celery root and rinse the roots under cold water, removing as much dirt as possible. Using a vegetable peeler or a paring knife, remove all the brown skin. Rinse the celery roots again, making sure they are cleaned of any skin. Cut each root into 8 pieces.

2. Put the celery root in a large stockpot, along with the onion, garlic, and bone broth. Bring the broth to a boil, reduce the heat to medium-high, and simmer until the celery root is softened, about 25 minutes. Strain the celery root mixture in a colander placed over a bowl, reserving the cooking liquid.

3. Return the celery root mixture to the stockpot and add the butter or ghee. Using a potato masher, mash the celery root with the onion and garlic. Transfer the mash to a blender or food processor and process until the celery root is whipped and creamy. If you are using a blender, be sure to remove the center cover from the lid and hold a towel over the hole to let some steam escape.

4. Add the coconut milk and process again. Add some of the reserved bone broth, 1 tablespoon at a time, and continue processing until the desired creaminess is achieved. Serve.

Zucchini Fritters

Makes 6 to 8 fritters

PREP
30 minutes (plus 1 hour resting time)

COOK
20 minutes

▶ In the winter, try replacing the zucchini with grated potato, cauliflower, or broccoli. If you are using potatoes, soak the grated potato in water for 1 hour before salting the vegetables as called for in step 1.

Latkes are a traditional Jewish dish made from potatoes and traditionally served at Hanukkah. These zucchini fritters are an adaptation of that time-honored favorite. Fried in pasture-raised lard, these fritters' appealing crispness always makes them a special treat. They create a perfect umami experience when paired with the Strawberry-Spiced Glazed Carrots (page 148) and the Chicken or Rabbit Mole (page 165).

2 large zucchini, grated
1 large white onion, grated
¾ teaspoon Celtic sea salt, divided
2 eggs
1 tablespoon bone broth of your choice (Chapter 3)
Pinch dried thyme
1 cup bread crumbs or gluten-free bread crumbs
½ cup shredded Parmesan (optional)
½ cup tallow

1. In a large bowl, combine the zucchini and onion, and then add ½ teaspoon of the salt. Toss thoroughly. Transfer to a colander set over a bowl and let drain for 20 minutes. Once or twice while resting, press the vegetables to extract as much liquid as possible.

2. In another bowl, beat together the eggs, bone broth, and thyme. Combine the drained vegetables with the egg mixture, and stir. Add the bread crumbs, Parmesan cheese (if using), and remaining ¼ teaspoon of salt, and stir to combine.

3. Scoop out ¼ cup of the mixture and, with your hands, shape into patties. Place the finished patties on a large plate. When all the patties are formed, cover and refrigerate them for 1 hour.

4. In a deep cast-iron pan, melt the tallow over medium-high heat. Place half of the patties in the pan and cook until golden brown and crisp, about 5 minutes per side.

5. Transfer the finished patties to a plate and cook the remaining patties. Serve.

Summer Vegetable Casserole

Serves 4 to 6

PREP
40 minutes

COOK
40 minutes

▶ This seasonal summer casserole can be served either cold as a main dish for brunch, or hot as a side dish for dinner.

This vegetable casserole is light in flavor but hearty and satisfying. If you have fresh herbs on hand, feel free to use them instead of dried ones. Make sure to slice the zucchini and eggplant at the same thickness, so they cook evenly. With its attractive presentation of layered vegetables and cheese, this dish is perfect for a potluck or buffet-style dinner party.

2 large eggplant, sliced
4 large zucchini, sliced
2 teaspoons Celtic sea salt, divided
1 cup bread crumbs or gluten-free bread crumbs
1 tablespoon dried basil
1 teaspoon freshly ground black pepper
1½ teaspoons dried oregano
3 cups shredded white Cheddar cheese, divided
4 large heirloom tomatoes, sliced
1 large white onion, sliced
½ cup bone broth of your choice (Chapter 3)
2 tablespoons pastured butter or ghee, cubed

1. In a large bowl, toss the eggplant and zucchini with 1 teaspoon of the salt. Let stand for 20 minutes and then rinse and pat dry with paper towels.

2. Preheat the oven to 350°F.

3. Combine the bread crumbs, basil, pepper, oregano, and remaining 1 teaspoon of salt in a bowl and mix to combine.

4. In a round baking dish, arrange a layer of eggplant and zucchini slices, spread out evenly over the bottom of the dish. Top with ¼ of the seasoned bread crumbs and ¾ cup of the cheese.

5. Add a layer of tomato slices and top it with another ¼ of the bread crumbs and ¾ cup cheese.

6. Add a layer of onion slices and top it with another ¼ of the bread crumbs and ¾ cup cheese. Use any remaining vegetables to create a final layer, and top with the remaining bread crumbs and cheese.

7. Pour the broth into the baking dish. Cover and bake until the vegetables are tender (insert a fork to test), about 30 minutes.

8. Uncover the dish and turn the oven to broil. Scatter the cubes of ghee or butter over the top of the dish. Broil until golden and bubbly, about 10 minutes. Serve.

Bacon and Cheddar Cauliflower Gratin

Serves 4 to 6

PREP
20 minutes

COOK
1 hour

▶ You can use any seasonal vegetable you have on hand for this recipe. Broccoli and potatoes both work particularly well, and are readily available choices that can stand up to a longer cook time.

A gratin is a great alternative to the usual mac and cheese. The word gratin *refers to the crust left behind after baking, and was usually reserved as a bonus for the chef. Rich and gooey, this gratin has plenty of crispy, creamy goodness, but replaces pasta with cauliflower, while substituting bone broth and coconut milk for the cream. This dish will undoubtedly win devoted fans thanks to the luxurious addition of melted cheddar and crispy bacon.*

8 bacon slices
1 head cauliflower, cored and cut into florets, leaves chopped
1 white onion, thinly sliced
2 garlic cloves, minced
⅔ cup bread crumbs or gluten-free bread crumbs
2 cups shredded raw Cheddar cheese, divided
¾ cup bone broth of your choice (Chapter 3)
¼ cup coconut milk
1 tablespoon ground turmeric

1. Preheat the oven to 375°F.

2. In a large skillet, cook the bacon until crisp. Transfer the bacon to a plate lined with paper towels. Drain off all but 2 teaspoons bacon fat from the pan and return it to the stove top. Chop the bacon and set aside.

3. Heat the bacon fat over medium heat and add the cauliflower florets and leaves, onion, and garlic. Cook, stirring frequently, until the onion becomes translucent and the cauliflower turns brown in spots, about 10 minutes. Remove the pan from the heat. Add the bacon, bread crumbs, and 1½ cups of the cheese to the pan, stirring to distribute evenly throughout. Transfer the mixture to a 9-inch baking dish.

CHAPTER 9

FROM LAND AND SEA

The inventive and delicious meat and seafood mains in this chapter promise to make bone broth a key ingredient on your dinner table. These recipes range from adapted classics you know and love to some of my favorite new creations. They also pair well with the vegetable recipes in chapter 8 if you would like to round out your protein with veggies. While I've suggested some of my favorite combinations, I also encourage you to mix and match as you please.

Fish Veracruzano

Serves 4 to 6

PREP
10 minutes

COOK
25 minutes

▶ Make the most of seasonal vegetables by adding them to this recipe as available. Asparagus, cauliflower, and green beans all go nicely with the flavors here.

Growing up by the beach in San Diego, I always ate plenty of fresh fish. When I was just a teenager, a friend of Mexican and Aztec descent taught me to prepare this dish, and we would make it for our friends who'd supply the daily catch. Hailing from the Veracruz region of Mexico, this recipe combines simmered tomatoes, onions, green olives, garlic, and raisins.

1 (2- to 3-pound) red snapper fillet (or other firm fish)
Celtic sea salt
Freshly ground black pepper
1½ cups Fish Bone Broth (page 56)
  or Chicken Bone Broth (page 41)
½ cup mayonnaise
1 cup diced tomato
1 large white onion, diced
1 cup pitted green olives
3 garlic cloves, minced
½ cup raisins

1. Preheat the oven to 375°F.

2. Season the snapper with salt and pepper and put in a baking dish.

3. In a small bowl, whisk together the bone broth and mayonnaise. Pour the mixture over the fish.

4. Add the tomato, onion, olives, garlic, and raisins to the dish. Cover with aluminum foil and bake for 25 minutes. Serve.

Herbed Mustard-Braised Chicken

Serves 6

PREP
10 minutes

COOK
1 hour 20 minutes

▶ Serve this dish with buttered green beans.

Chicken thighs are my favorite part of the chicken—thanks to their fat content, they're very hard to overcook and have a silkier texture than other parts of the bird. In this simple dish they are braised in a classic mix of broth, herbs, and mustard. If you prefer to use boneless, skinless chicken thighs, just reduce the cooking time by half.

1 cup Chicken Bone Broth (page 41)
¼ cup whole-grain mustard
1 teaspoon dried thyme
1 teaspoon dried rosemary
1 tablespoon chicken fat
6 bone-in, skin-on chicken thighs
Celtic sea salt
Freshly ground black pepper
1 onion, thinly sliced
2 garlic cloves, minced
2 tablespoons raw honey
1 tablespoon ghee, tallow, or lard

1. Preheat the oven to 350°F.

2. In a measuring cup, whisk together the broth, mustard, thyme, and rosemary and set aside.

3. In a large cast-iron Dutch oven, heat the chicken fat over medium-high heat.

4. Season the chicken thighs with salt and pepper and put in the pot. Brown well, 3 to 5 minutes per side. Remove the thighs from the pot and set aside.

5. Add the onion and garlic to the pot and cook until fragrant and beginning to soften. Pour the broth mixture into the pot. Bring to a simmer, and return the chicken thighs to the pot. Cover the pot and bake in the oven until the juices run clear, about 1 hour. Every 10 minutes, baste the chicken thighs with the cooking liquid.

6. Remove the chicken thighs from the pot and arrange on a serving tray. Place the pot back on the stove and add the honey, stirring to combine. Bring the mixture to a boil and then reduce the heat to a simmer. Reduce the sauce by half and then add the ghee, stirring until it melts. Pour the sauce over the thighs and serve.

Chicken Liver Pâté

Makes 1¼ pounds

PREP
10 minutes (plus at
least 5 hours chilling
and resting time)

COOK
10 minutes

▶ If you have picky
eaters who are
particular about the
taste of liver, omit the
tallow and use bacon
fat, which has a smoky
(and sneaky) flavor.

*Pâté dates back all the way to ancient Greece, where it was made from a
variety of different meats, preserved in salt, and sold on street corners to
both the rich and the poor. While classic versions include butter or cream,
this version uses only ghee and coconut milk.*

6 tablespoons melted ghee, tallow, or lard, divided
1 pound pastured chicken livers
3 tablespoons brandy, divided
1 small white onion, finely chopped
1 small fennel bulb, cored and chopped
½ cup bone broth of your choice (Chapter 3)
3 tablespoons full-fat coconut milk
1 teaspoon Celtic sea salt
½ teaspoon ground allspice
¼ teaspoon freshly ground black pepper
⅛ teaspoon ground nutmeg

1. In a large cast-iron skillet, heat 2 tablespoons of the ghee or tallow
over medium-high heat. Sauté the chicken livers for 1 minute on each
side. While the livers are cooking, add 2 tablespoons of the brandy to
the pan. Remove the livers with a slotted spoon and set aside.

2. Add the onion and fennel to the skillet. Cook until the vegetables
just begin to soften. Add the remaining 1 tablespoon of brandy to the
skillet and continue to cook until the vegetables become translucent,
about 8 minutes more.

3. Transfer the onion, fennel, and livers to a food processor.

4. Pour the bone broth into the skillet and swirl it around to remove any
leftover bits in the pan. Transfer the broth to a measuring cup. Add the
coconut milk, remaining 4 tablespoons of melted ghee or tallow, salt,
allspice, pepper, and nutmeg to the measuring cup. Whisk to combine.

5. Pulse the liver-onion-fennel mixture until roughly chopped. With
the food processor running, slowly pour the broth mixture through the
feed tube and process until the mixture is smooth and creamy.

6. Transfer the pâté to a ramekin, cover, and chill for at least 4 hours
before serving. Remove from the refrigerator 1 hour before serving.

Grammy Bee's Fried Chicken

Serves 4

PREP

5 minutes (plus at least 12 hours brining time)

COOK

45 minutes

► If you don't have a candy thermometer to measure the oil temperature, that's okay, too. Heat the oil over medium-high heat and test it for readiness by dropping a dash of flour into it. When it quickly sizzles and disappears, the oil is ready to go. If it lingers on the surface, wait a couple of minutes and try again.

I have wonderful childhood memories of my grandmother's fried chicken, equally delicious served piping hot or straight from the refrigerator. Grammy Bee was from the Appalachian mountains of North Carolina and always kept a mug of bacon grease next to her stove. I prepare my fried chicken the same way she did, in a cast-iron pan that is a treasured family heirloom.

2 quarts water
1 cup Celtic sea salt, plus more for the flour
¼ cup freshly ground black pepper, plus more for the flour
3 tablespoons cayenne pepper, plus more for the flour
3 tablespoons garlic powder
3 tablespoons onion powder
1 (3½- to 4-pound) chicken, cut into 8 pieces
2½ cups lard
3 cups all-purpose flour or gluten-free flour

1. In a large bowl or pot, combine the water, 1 cup salt, ¼ cup black pepper, 3 tablespoons cayenne, garlic powder, and onion powder to create a brine. Mix well and submerge the chicken pieces in the brine. Cover and refrigerate overnight.

2. The following day, remove the chicken pieces from the brine. Pat the chicken dry using paper towels.

3. In a large, deep pot, heat the lard over medium-high heat to 350°F. Preheat the oven to 250°F.

4. In a large paper bag, add the flour and season with salt, pepper, and cayenne. Put 1 piece of chicken in the bag at a time, close the top, and shake to coat. Remove the chicken from the bag and set on a wire rack. Repeat with the remaining chicken pieces. ▶

Grammy Bee's Fried Chicken continued

5. Carefully lower a few pieces of chicken into the hot lard and fry until golden brown, 10 to 12 minutes per side. Do not crowd the chicken. Flip the chicken once while frying to ensure that each side is cooked evenly and browns well.

6. As each piece of chicken is done, use tongs to remove it from the pot and place it on a baking sheet in the warm oven. Cook the remaining chicken in the same manner. Serve.

Duck Larb

Serves 4

PREP
10 minutes

COOK
5 minutes

▶ Replace the duck with chicken, pork, shrimp, or beef for an equally delicious meal.

Larb is a traditional Laotian dish that can be made with many varieties of meat. If you hunt for ducks yourself, or know a duck hunter, this is an easy and fun way to prepare and enjoy it. If you don't have access to wild ducks, you can easily find whole roast ducks in Chinese delis, or simply order one from your local butcher shop.

½ teaspoon tallow
1 small onion, chopped
½ cup chopped roasted peanuts (optional)
½ cup chopped fresh mint
½ cup shredded unsweetened coconut
1 recipe Spicy Asian Dressing (page 105)
Meat from 1 cooked duck, shredded
Lettuce leaves, for serving

1. In a medium skillet, heat the tallow over medium heat. Remove the pan from the heat. Add the onion, peanuts (if using), mint, and coconut, tossing to combine.

2. Arrange the duck meat on individual plates and drizzle the Spicy Asian Dressing over the meat. Garnish with the peanut-mint-coconut mixture. Serve with lettuce leaves for scooping.

Classic Bone Marrow and Dressed Microgreens

Serves 4

PREP
10 minutes

COOK
25 minutes

▶ No need to stick to just beef bones for this simple, yet nutritious recipe. For an alternative but equally rich flavor, try a variety of bones such as lamb, pork, or game.

Bone marrow served in the bone is a delicacy and a luscious treat. Because of its high fat content, it's occasionally referred to as "meat butter." Spread the marrow on your favorite toasted bread, with a topping of parsley, touches of salt, and briny capers to brighten the dish.

4 (8- to 10-inch) marrowbones, cut into 2-inch rounds
  (make sure your butcher does this for you)
1 cup chopped fresh parsley
1 small shallot, chopped
1 tablespoon capers, chopped
2 tablespoons olive oil, divided
2 tablespoons apple cider vinegar, divided
1½ cups microgreens
2 radishes, thinly sliced
Celtic sea salt
Freshly ground black pepper
12 baguette slices, toasted

1. Preheat the oven to 450°F.

2. Place the bones, cut-side down, in a cast-iron skillet or roasting pan. Roast the bones until the marrow is soft and beginning to separate from the bones but before it begins to melt, 15 to 20 minutes.

3. In a small bowl, combine the parsley, shallot, capers, 1½ tablespoons of the olive oil, and 1½ tablespoons of the apple cider vinegar.

4. In a bowl, dress the microgreens and radishes with the remaining ½ tablespoon of olive oil and ½ tablespoon of apple cider vinegar. Season with salt and pepper.

5. Divide the marrowbones among four plates. Spoon some of the parsley mixture on each marrowbone. Serve with the dressed microgreens and toasted baguette slices. Use a long, thin spoon to scoop the marrow onto the toasts.

Braised Lamb with Preserved Lemons and Bourbon Fruit Chutney

Serves 4

PREP
5 minutes

COOK
2 hours

This is one of my favorite recipes. The lamb is prepared simply, with classic ingredients including fresh rosemary, whole garlic cloves, and the chopped rind of preserved lemons. Preserved lemons are easy to make at home, and wonderful to have on hand for adding to any dish. Braise the lamb until it is fork-tender and easily pulls away from the bone.

1 pound lamb shoulder
Celtic sea salt
1 tablespoon tallow
6 fresh rosemary sprigs
6 garlic cloves, peeled
1¼ cups bone broth of your choice (Chapter 3), divided
1 tablespoon apple cider vinegar
¼ cup preserved lemon rind, cut into slices
½ cup Bourbon Fruit Chutney (page 109)

1. Preheat the oven to 325°F.

2. Season the lamb shoulder with salt. Using a sharp knife, score the fat cap on the shoulder several times.

3. In a cast-iron pan, heat the tallow over medium-high heat. Sear the lamb shoulder until well browned on all sides.

4. Tuck the rosemary sprigs under the lamb, and add the garlic cloves to the pan.

5. Pour 1 cup of the bone broth over the lamb. Add the apple cider vinegar and lemon rind to the pan. Cover the pan with a lid or aluminum foil and bake until the broth has completely evaporated and the meat pulls away from the bone, about 1½ hours.

6. Transfer the lamb to a serving platter. Tent loosely with foil and let rest for 15 minutes.

7. Discard the rosemary sprigs and garlic cloves. Add the remaining ¼ cup of bone broth and the Bourbon Fruit Chutney to the pan and heat over medium-high heat, scraping the bottom of the pan as you mix the two together. Bring the sauce to a simmer, pour over the lamb, and serve.

Braised Lamb Shanks with Polenta

Serves 4

PREP
20 minutes

COOK
Slow Cooker:
6 hours

▶ You can also use beef or pork shanks for this recipe.

Lamb shanks must be gently cooked for a long time, until they become fork-tender and the meat falls off the bone. Polenta has roots going back as far as Roman times: the word itself actually means "porridge," and it was originally made from slow-cooked millet or spelt. It wasn't until corn was introduced to Europe in the seventeenth century that polenta developed into the corn-based dish we know today.

FOR THE LAMB SHANKS
Marrow from 1 roasted marrowbone (see page 99)
2 carrots, chopped
2 celery stalks, chopped
1 onion, chopped
3 garlic cloves, minced
2 cups Lamb Bone Broth (page 46), Beef Bone Broth (page 39),
  or Chicken Bone Broth (page 41)
1 cup peeled, seeded, chopped tomatoes
2 tablespoons tomato paste
1 teaspoon chopped fresh thyme
1 bay leaf
4 lamb shanks, trimmed of excess fat
Celtic sea salt
Freshly ground black pepper
2 tablespoons tallow
1 cup dry red wine
¼ cup apple cider vinegar

FOR THE POLENTA
5 to 6 cups Chicken Bone Broth (page 41)
  or Beef Bone Broth (page 39)
1 cup medium to fine cornmeal
¼ cup ghee, tallow, or lard
1 teaspoon Celtic sea salt
1 teaspoon freshly ground black pepper

TO MAKE THE LAMB SHANKS

1. In a small pan, melt the marrow and then transfer it to a slow cooker.

2. Add the carrots, celery, onion, garlic, bone broth, tomatoes, tomato paste, thyme, and bay leaf to the slow cooker and stir to combine.

3. Season the lamb shanks with salt and pepper. In a large sauté pan warm the tallow over medium-high heat until nearly smoking. Add the shanks and brown on all sides, about 5 minutes total. Transfer to the slow cooker.

4. Remove the sauté pan from the heat, pour in the wine to deglaze the pan, and return it to medium-high heat. Bring the wine to a simmer, stirring to scrape up any browned bits from the bottom of the pan. Add the wine glaze and apple cider vinegar to the slow cooker. Cover and cook on high for 6 hours. Transfer the lamb shanks to a large serving dish.

5. Remove the bay leaf from the slow cooker. Using a countertop blender or immersion blender, purée the contents of the slow cooker until smooth. Pour some of the sauce over the shanks and serve the rest alongside.

TO MAKE THE POLENTA

1. When the lamb is nearly done, in a medium saucepan, bring 5 cups of the bone broth to a boil over high heat.

2. Pour the cornmeal slowly into the bone broth, whisking to combine. Continue to whisk as the mixture thickens, 2 to 3 minutes.

3. Turn the heat to low. Simmer for 45 minutes, stirring every 10 minutes or so. If the polenta becomes too thick, thin it with an additional ½ cup bone broth, stirring to combine, and continue cooking. Add up to 1 cup more of bone broth if necessary, to keep the polenta soft enough to stir.

4. Stir in the ghee, salt, and pepper. Serve with the lamb shanks.

Braised Lamb Pappardelle with Mint, Peas, and Baby Artichokes

Serves 4

PREP
5 minutes

COOK
20 minutes

▶ For a lighter alternative, substitute seasonal vegetables for the lamb meat.

I love to make this recipe in the spring when I have leftover braised lamb. The elements of mint, fresh peas, artichokes, and lemon zest add a bright, zingy flavor to the gamy meat. Find both fresh peas and baby artichokes at your local farmers' market. To prepare the baby artichokes, simply snap off the dark outer leaves until you reach the pale yellow ones inside, and trim off any dark parts of the stem as well.

1 pound pappardelle
1 tablespoon ghee, tallow, or lard
½ cup Lamb Bone Broth (page 46)
2 cups shredded cooked lamb
1½ cups fresh peas
8 baby artichokes, steamed and quartered
½ cup chopped fresh mint
¼ cup grated lemon zest
Celtic sea salt
Freshly ground black pepper

1. Cook the pappardelle according to the package directions. Drain and transfer to a serving bowl. Toss the pappardelle with the ghee and set aside.

2. In a medium saucepan, combine the Lamb Bone Broth, lamb meat, peas, and artichokes. Bring to a simmer over medium heat, stirring well.

3. Add the lamb mixture to the pappardelle. Add the mint and lemon zest and mix well. Season with salt and pepper and serve.

Pork Agrodolce
(Sweet and Sour Pork)

Serves 6 to 8

PREP
10 minutes

COOK
25 minutes

▶ This sweet and sour sauce is great on fish, chicken, meats, and vegetables on their own.

Agrodolce is an Italian word that literally means "bitter and sweet," but the flavor profile can actually be found in multiple cuisines, including the classic sweet and sour dishes of China. While Italians love to pair this sauce with game meats, I chose to prepare it here in the Chinese style, much like a stir-fry, but with traditional Italian ingredients including raisins, pine nuts, and balsamic vinegar. I recommend serving it with buttery sprouted brown rice.

1 tablespoon tallow
1½ pounds pork loin or boneless pork chops, cut into strips
1 garlic clove, minced
1 red onion, sliced
1 white onion, sliced 3 cups sliced bell pepper (mixed colors)
½ cup raisins
½ cup bone broth of your choice (Chapter 3)
¼ cup balsamic vinegar
¼ cup apple cider vinegar
3 tablespoons raw cane sugar
½ cup pine nuts

1. In a medium skillet, heat the tallow over medium-high heat. Add the pork and stir-fry until the meat becomes white.

2. Add the garlic and stir to combine. Add the onions and peppers and stir to combine. Cook the mixture until the onions become soft and translucent, about 15 minutes.

3. Add the raisins to the pan and stir to combine.

4. In a small bowl, whisk together the bone broth, balsamic vinegar, apple cider vinegar, and sugar.

5. Turn the heat up to high and add the vinegar mixture. Bring to a boil and stir continuously until the sauce has reduced and is coating the meat and vegetables.

6. Add the pine nuts, toss well, and serve.

Apple Butter and Ale Pork Ribs with Sweet Potatoes

Serves 4 to 6

PREP
5 minutes

COOK
1 hour 15 minutes

▶ This pork is also great cold! Chill it overnight and add it to your favorite autumnal salad.

Unlike other types of spareribs, country-style ribs are cut from the sirloin end of the loin and are generally sold boneless. In this recipe the meaty ribs are braised in a delicious blend of warming apple butter and your favorite ale, along with ginger, onions, and sweet potato. The results melt in your mouth with the sweet and savory flavors of fall.

2 cups sweet potato slices
1½ teaspoons lard
1½ pounds country-style pork ribs
¼ cup chopped onion
1 thin slice fresh ginger
1 recipe Apple Butter–Ale Sauce (page 110)

1. Preheat the oven to 325°F.

2. Bring a medium saucepan of water to a boil over medium-high heat. Add the sweet potato slices to the water and parboil, 4 to 5 minutes.

3. Drain the parboiled sweet potatoes and arrange them in a baking dish; set aside.

4. In a large skillet, heat the lard over medium-high heat. Sear the pork ribs until browned on both sides and transfer to the baking dish.

5. Add the onion, ginger, and Apple Butter–Ale Sauce. Cook, uncovered, for 1 hour. Serve.

Pomegranate-Glazed Short Ribs

Serves 4

PREP
10 minutes

COOK
2 hours

▶ Serve these short ribs with Whipped Celery Root (page 154).

This is a showstopping dish and an excellent main course for special occasions or holidays. Short ribs have become a restaurant favorite in recent years, often braised in red wine. This recipe is rich and complex thanks to the addition of pomegranate jelly, which adds acidity to balance the meatiness of the dish. Because they contain meat, fat, and bone, short ribs require a long time to cook, so plan accordingly.

1½ cups bone broth of your choice (Chapter 3)

1 cup pomegranate jelly

2½ pounds beef short ribs

Celtic sea salt

Freshly ground black pepper

1 tablespoon tallow

2 cups chopped white onion

1 large carrot, chopped

1½ cups chopped celery

2 cups sliced shiitake mushrooms

1 tomato, diced

1½ cups dry red wine

1 large rosemary sprig

3 thyme sprigs

3 garlic cloves, minced

1. Preheat the oven to 350°F.

2. In a small saucepan, heat the bone broth and pomegranate jelly over medium heat. Whisk until combined and the jelly dissolves, and then turn off the heat.

3. Season the short ribs with salt and pepper.

4. In a large, ovenproof pot, heat the tallow over medium-high heat. Brown the short ribs on all sides, 2 to 3 minutes per side. Transfer them to a plate and set aside. ▶

Pomegranate-Glazed
Short Ribs continued

5. Add the onion, carrot, celery, and mushrooms to the pot and cook, stirring, until the onion begins to soften, about 5 minutes.

6. Add the tomato and cook, stirring constantly, for 3 minutes. Pour in the wine and the bone broth–jelly mixture, scraping the bottom of the pan with a spatula as you add the liquid.

7. Return the short ribs to the pot. Bring to a boil, lower the heat to medium, and simmer until the liquid has reduced by half, about 25 minutes.

8. Add the rosemary, thyme, and garlic to the pot. Bring to a boil, cover, and transfer to the oven.

9. Cook until the short ribs are tender and the meat is pulling away from the bones, about 1½ hours, and transfer them to a platter.

10. Stir the remaining sauce in the pan and season it with salt and pepper. Spoon the sauce over the short ribs and serve.

Pot Roast

Serves 6

PREP
15 minutes

COOK
3 hours and 15 minutes

Perfect for a family dinner on a chilly winter weekend, pot roast is the definition of comfort food. I've given this dish a sophisticated twist by adding sherry and tart cherry jam, while offering the warm fondness of the classic. For a more traditional version, replace the sherry with a robust red wine like Zinfandel or Syrah.

Salt and freshly ground black pepper
3 pounds grass fed chuck roast
3 tablespoons tallow, lard, or ghee, divided
4–6 medium carrots, cut into 1-inch pieces
2 white onions, quartered
6 red or new potatoes, quartered (omit for Paleo option)
3 sprigs rosemary
4 peeled and whole garlic cloves
4 cups bone broth of your choice (Chapter 3)
¾ cup dry sherry
2 tablespoons tart cherry jam

1. Preheat the oven to 275°.

2. Generously season the roast with salt and pepper.

3. In a large Dutch oven, heat 1 tablespoon of tallow on medium high heat. Add the carrots, onions, potatoes, rosemary, and garlic to the pot and cook for 5 to 7 minutes. Remove from the pan and reserve.

4. Add 2 tablespoons of tallow to the pot and sear your meat until browned, about 1 minute on each side. Remove from the pan and reserve.

5. Add the bone broth, sherry, and jam into the pot over medium heat, scraping the bottom, stirring to combine.

6. Once the broth has been combined, add the meat and vegetables back to the pot. Place the lid on the pot and transfer it to the oven for about 3 hours. The roast is ready when it easily falls apart with a fork.

DESSERTS

What's a cookbook without a desserts chapter? I hope by now you have been pleasantly surprised at how versatile bone broth can be. I'm finishing off this book with five scrumptious dessert recipes that prove broth can add amazing flavor to sweets as well. As with "brothtails," desserts shouldn't be the only way you add broth to your diet, but they can make delightful treats for a special occasions.

Zucchini Bread

Makes 1 loaf

PREP
20 minutes

COOK
1 hour

▶ For even more flavor, add 1 cup of your favorite chopped, dried fruit to this recipe. Dates, raisins, and figs all make great additions to this quick bread.

Delicious and simple-to-make zucchini quick bread is extremely versatile. You can serve it as a dessert with ice cream or clotted cream, in place of a breakfast pastry, or as an afternoon snack. I particularly enjoy it slathered in rich pastured butter and served with coffee. It also makes a lovely holiday or hostess gift.

2 cups shredded zucchini, drained

1 egg

½ cup pastured butter, melted

½ cup neutral bone broth of your choice (page 38)

½ cup coconut milk

1 cup raw cane sugar

1 teaspoon pure vanilla extract

1½ cups all-purpose flour

1 teaspoon baking soda

1 teaspoon ground cinnamon

1 teaspoon ground turmeric

1 teaspoon ground nutmeg

1½ teaspoons grated fresh ginger

1 cup chopped walnuts, lightly toasted

1. Preheat the oven to 350°F.

2. In a large bowl, mix the zucchini, egg, butter, bone broth, coconut milk, sugar, and vanilla. Stir to combine.

3. In another bowl, mix the flour, baking soda, cinnamon, turmeric, nutmeg, and ginger. Stir to combine. Add the dry mixture to the wet mixture and mix until there are no flour clumps. Fold in the walnuts.

4. Pour the bread batter into a greased loaf pan and bake until the top of the bread is browned and an inserted utensil comes out clean, about 1 hour.

Ginger Cookies

Makes 3 dozen

PREP
20 minutes
(plus 20 minutes
chilling time)

COOK
15 minutes

Spicy and sweet ginger cookies make a pleasant end to a meal. Warming fall spices cinnamon, allspice, and nutmeg complement the bite of fresh ginger in this richly flavored treat. Serve with hot herbal tea or a hot bone broth drink such as the Cinnamon Roll (page 76).

1 cup pastured butter
1½ cups raw cane sugar
2 eggs
¼ cup neutral bone broth of your choice (page 38)
½ teaspoon pure vanilla extract
2¾ cups whole-wheat flour
1 teaspoon baking soda
½ teaspoon Celtic sea salt
½ teaspoon ground cinnamon
¼ teaspoon ground allspice
¼ teaspoon ground nutmeg
2 tablespoons grated fresh ginger

1. Preheat the oven to 350°F.

2. Using an electric mixer, cream the butter and sugar until it becomes light and fluffy.

3. With the mixer running on low, add the eggs, bone broth, and vanilla and continue mixing until well incorporated.

4. In a separate bowl, mix the flour, baking soda, salt, cinnamon, allspice, nutmeg, and ginger. Add the flour mixture to the mixer and continue mixing on low until well incorporated.

5. Transfer the dough to the refrigerator to chill for 20 minutes.

6. Scoop tablespoon-size balls of dough onto a cookie sheet.

7. Bake until the cookies achieve the texture you prefer, 8 minutes for cakier, fluffier cookies and up to 14 minutes for crisp cookies.

Berry Cobbler

Serves 8 to 10

PREP
30 minutes

COOK
1 hour

▶ Make this a seasonal dish by using whatever fruit you have on hand. Substitute peaches, plums, or even grapes for the berries in this recipe for a different take on this simple cobbler.

It might come as a surprise that it's possible to make a berry cobbler with bone broth. The berries absorb the broth nicely, while the vanilla helps mask even the slightest beefy flavor. You can use a single type of berry, but a mixture such as raspberries, blueberries, and blackberries will be even more delicious. Serve this warm from the oven with whipped coconut cream.

FOR THE FILLING

3½ cups mixed berries

1 cup raw cane sugar

1 cup neutral bone broth of your choice (page 38)

½ teaspoon pure vanilla extract

½ teaspoon ground cinnamon

FOR THE COBBLER

¾ cup all-purpose flour

3 tablespoons raw cane sugar

1 teaspoon baking powder

½ teaspoon Celtic sea salt

¼ teaspoon baking soda

6 tablespoons cold pastured butter, cubed

¼ cup neutral bone broth of your choice (page 38)

TO MAKE THE FILLING

1. In a medium pot, combine the berries, sugar, bone broth, vanilla, and cinnamon. Bring to a boil over medium-high heat.

2. Reduce the heat and simmer until thickened, about 25 minutes. Remove from the heat and set aside. ▶

Berry Cobbler continued

TO MAKE THE COBBLER

1. Preheat the oven to 350°F.

2. In a large bowl, combine the flour, sugar, baking powder, salt, and baking soda. Cut in the butter using a pastry knife until the mixture is in pea-size pieces. Fold in the bone broth. Place in the refrigerator to chill for 15 minutes.

3. Pour the berry mixture into a 9-inch pie dish. Break off pieces of the dough and scatter them over the top until the berries are covered.

4. Bake until the top of the cobbler is golden brown, 30 to 35 minutes. Serve warm.

Kahlúa Brownies

Makes 12 brownies

PREP
15 minutes

COOK
45 minutes

These brownies are perfectly dense, fudgy, and packed with chocolate flavor. You would never guess that they include bone broth. A hint of coffee liqueur enhances the chocolate flavor, but you can replace that with brewed coffee, a different-flavored liqueur such as Grand Marnier, or with rum. Kids absolutely love these rich treats.

6 tablespoons pastured butter
⅓ cup neutral bone broth of your choice (page 38)
⅓ cup coconut milk
¾ cup plus 2 tablespoons unsweetened cocoa powder
1¼ cups raw cane sugar
¼ teaspoon Celtic sea salt
2 eggs
½ teaspoon pure vanilla extract
2 tablespoons Kahlúa
¾ cup all-purpose flour
½ cup chocolate chips

1. Preheat the oven to 350°F.

2. In a metal bowl, combine the butter, bone broth, coconut milk, cocoa powder, sugar, and salt.

3. In a medium saucepan, bring a few inches of water to a boil over medium heat. Place the bowl over the saucepan and, stirring constantly, cook until the mixture is heated through and becomes glossy, 10 to 15 minutes. Take off the heat and let rest for 15 minutes.

4. Stir in the eggs, one at a time. Add the vanilla and Kahlúa.

5. Fold the flour into the mixture until no flour is visible. Add the chocolate chips and mix well.

6. Pour the batter into a greased 9-inch pan and bake for 35 minutes.

Sweet Potato Pie

Serves 6 to 8

PREP

20 minutes (plus
at least 30 minutes
chilling time)

COOK

50 minutes

▶ For added flair,
arrange halved pecans
in a pinwheel around
the center of the pie.

Pie is always a delicious indulgence. In the case of sweet potato pie, at least, it comes with some health benefits to counter the sugar and fat. Flavored with bourbon and raw honey, this pie is perfect for the Thanksgiving table. Using both lard and butter yields a crust at once crisp and flavorful—the flakiness is produced by leaving small lumps of fat, so resist the urge to create a smooth, uniform dough.

FOR THE CRUST

1¾ cups all-purpose flour

1 tablespoon raw cane sugar

¼ teaspoon Celtic sea salt

6 tablespoons pastured butter

6 tablespoons lard

3 tablespoons neutral bone broth of your choice (page 38)

FOR THE FILLING

2 cups mashed cooked sweet potato

½ cup raw honey

2 eggs

2 tablespoons bourbon

TO MAKE THE CRUST

1. In a large bowl, mix the flour, sugar, and salt. Using a pastry knife, cut in the butter and lard until it is in pea-size pieces.

2. Add the bone broth to the flour mixture 1 tablespoon at a time, folding the mixture with a spatula after each addition. Once the broth is added and mixed well, the crust will hold together. Form the dough into a disc, cover with plastic wrap, and chill for 30 minutes to 1 hour.

3. Preheat the oven to 350°F.

4. Roll out the dough disc and shape it into a large circle. Fit it into a 9-inch pie pan and fold and pinch the edges.

5. Cover the inner surface of the pie with a piece of parchment paper, and weight the pie crust using dried beans or pie weights to hold the crust in place.

6. Bake the crust until lightly browned and slightly crumbly at the edges, about 25 minutes.

TO MAKE THE FILLING

1. In a food processor, combine the sweet potato, honey, eggs, and bourbon. Process to combine.

2. Pour the filling into the baked pie crust and bake until set, about 25 minutes. Cool to room temperature and serve.

Seasonal Vegetable Guide

Using in-season vegetables is the easiest way to get fresh and nutritious produce at an affordable price. Many of the recipes in this book are designed to include seasonal vegetables, giving you the freedom to use the ingredients that are more readily available at a particular time of year. These fresh veggies are always a lot tastier, too. Plus, you'll be able to make the same recipe a little different every time, keeping things exciting and satisfying as the seasons change. This is a list of each season's greatest hits, designed to jump-start your creativity. Feel free to experiment with other seasonal options you find at your local grocery store, co-op, or farmers' market.

Winter

Beets, broccoli, cabbage, carrots, cauliflower, celery, kale, onions, radishes, winter squash.

Spring

Artichokes, arugula, asparagus, broccoli, cabbage, carrots, fennel, mustard greens, spinach, spring peas.

Summer

Cantaloupe, corn, cucumbers, eggplant, green beans, okra, radishes, summer squash, sweet and spicy peppers.

Fall

Butter lettuce, endive, kohlrabi, pumpkins, radicchio, sweet potato, swiss chard, turnips, winter squash.

The Dirty Dozen
and the Clean Fifteen

A nonprofit and environmental watchdog organization called Environmental Working Group (EWG) looks at data supplied by the US Department of Agriculture (USDA) and the US Food and Drug Administration (FDA) about pesticide residues, and compiles a list each year of the best and worst pesticide loads found in commercial crops. You can refer to the Dirty Dozen list to know which fruits and vegetables you should always buy organic. The Clean Fifteen list lets you know which produce is considered safe enough when grown conventionally to allow you to skip the organics. This does not mean that the Clean Fifteen produce is pesticide-free, so wash these fruits and vegetables thoroughly. These lists change every year, so make sure you look up the most recent before you fill your shopping cart. You'll find the most recent lists as well as a guide to pesticides in produce at EWG.org/FoodNews.

2015

DIRTY DOZEN	CLEAN FIFTEEN
Apples	Asparagus
Celery	Avocados
Cherry tomatoes	Cabbage
Cucumbers	Cantaloupe
Grapes	Cauliflower
Nectarines	Eggplant
Peaches	Grapefruit
Potatoes	Kiwis
Snap peas	Mangos
Spinach	Onions
Strawberries	Papayas
Sweet bell peppers	Pineapples
	Sweet corn
	Sweet peas (frozen)
	Sweet potatoes

In addition to the Dirty Dozen, the EWG added two foods contaminated with highly toxic organophosphate insecticides:

Hot peppers
Kale/Collard greens

Conversion Tables

Volume Equivalents (Liquid)

US STANDARD	US STANDARD (OUNCES)	METRIC (APPROXIMATE)
2 tablespoons	1 fl. oz.	30 mL
¼ cup	2 fl. oz.	60 mL
½ cup	4 fl. oz.	120 mL
1 cup	8 fl. oz.	240 mL
1½ cups	12 fl. oz.	355 mL
2 cups or 1 pint	16 fl. oz.	475 mL
4 cups or 1 quart	32 fl. oz.	1 L
1 gallon	128 fl. oz.	4 L

Oven Temperatures

FAHRENHEIT (F)	CELSIUS (C) (APPROXIMATE)
250°F	120°C
300°F	150°C
325°F	165°C
350°F	180°C
375°F	190°C
400°F	200°C
425°F	220°C
450°F	230°C

Volume Equivalents (Dry)

US STANDARD	METRIC (APPROXIMATE)
⅛ teaspoon	0.5 mL
¼ teaspoon	1 mL
½ teaspoon	2 mL
¾ teaspoon	4 mL
1 teaspoon	5 mL
1 tablespoon	15 mL
¼ cup	59 mL
⅓ cup	79 mL
½ cup	118 mL
⅔ cup	156 mL
¾ cup	177 mL
1 cup	235 mL
2 cups or 1 pint	475 mL
3 cups	700 mL
4 cups or 1 quart	1 L
½ gallon	2 L
1 gallon	4 L

Weight Equivalents

US STANDARD	METRIC (APPROXIMATE)
½ ounce	15 g
1 ounce	30 g
2 ounces	60 g
4 ounces	115 g
8 ounces	225 g
12 ounces	340 g
16 ounces or 1 pound	455 g

Resources

Cookware

lecreuset.com (enameled cast-iron cookware)
lodgemfg.com (cast-iron cookware)
staubusa.com (enameled cast-iron cookware)

Dairy Products

barnandbutter.com (dairy resource)
omghee.com (ghee)
organicpastures.com (raw dairy)
springhillbutter.com (pasture-raised
farmstead butter and cheese products)

Educational Resources

animalwelfareapproved.org
farmtoconsumer.org
reviveandthrive.com
specialtyproduce.com
westonaprice.org

Herbs and Spices

mountainroseherbs.com
worldspice.com

Pastured and Ethically Raised Animals

cookspigs.com (pasture-raised heritage pigs)
cop.com Catalina Offshore Products
(high-quality sushi-grade seafood)
da-le-ranch.com (pasture-raised cattle,
pigs, and poultry)
homegrownmeats.com (pasture-raised cattle)
lajollabutchershop.com (full-service butcher)
openspacemeats.com (pasture-raised cattle)
sagemountainbeef.com (pasture-raised
cattle)
uswellnessmeats.com (pasture-raised
animals and health products)

References

"3 First Foods That Your Baby Needs." *Holistic Squid*. Accessed August 19, 2015. holisticsquid.com/3-first-foods-that-your-baby-needs/

"5 Healing Effects of Lavender." *Health.com*. Accessed September 7, 2015. www.health.com/health/gallery/0,,20587573_4,00.html

"16 Health Benefits of Drinking Warm Lemon Water Everyday." *Food Matters*. Accessed September 7, 2015. foodmatters.tv/articles-1/cheers-to-drinking-warm-lemon-water

"Arthritis Diet." *Arthritis Foundation*. Accessed August 28, 2015. www.arthritis.org/living-with-arthritis/arthritis-diet/

Baird, Sarah. "How Bone Broth Got Its Early Start from Beef Tea in the 1800s." *Eater*. Accessed August 20, 2015. www.eater.com/drinks/2015/5/20/8626891/how-bone-broth-got-its-early-start-from-beef-tea-in-the-1800s

"The Benefits of Bone Broth in Traditional Chinese Medicine." *Osso Good Bones*. Accessed August 23, 2015. blog.ossogoodbones.com/benefits-bone-broth-traditional-chinese-medicine/

Berman, Ali. "5 Herbs for Beautiful Skin." *Mother Nature News*. Accessed August 29, 2015. www.mnn.com/lifestyle/natural-beauty-fashion/stories/5-herbs-for-beautiful-skin

"Chamomile: An Herbal Medicine of the Past with a Bright Future." *US National Library of Medicine National Institutes of Health*. Accessed September 5, 2015. www.ncbi.nlm.nih.gov/pmc/articles/PMC2995283/

"Code of Federal Regulations –Title 21." *US Food and Drug Administration*. Accessed August 23, 2015. www.accessdata.fda.gov/scripts/cdrh/cfdocs/cfcfr/cfrsearch.cfm?fr=501.22

Culinary Dictionary. *What's Cooking America*. Accessed November 3, 2015. www.whatscookingamerica.net

Fallon, Sally and Mary Enig. *Nourishing Traditions: The Cookbook that Challenges Politically Correct Nutrition and the Diet Dictocrats*. White Plains, DC: NewTrends Publishing, Inc, 2003.

"Ginger Root as a Sleeping Remedy." Livestrong. Accessed September 6, 2015. www.livestrong.com/article/534287-ginger-root-as-a-sleeping-remedy/

"Guide to Buying Grass Fed Beef." Rodale's Organic Life. Accessed August 22, 2015. www.rodalesorganiclife.com/food/grassfed-beef

"Healing Leaky Gut Syndrome." *Women to Women*. Accessed August 21, 2015. www.womentowomen.com/digestive-health/healing-leaky-gut-syndrome-open-the-door-to-good-health-2/

"Herbs for the Mom to Be." *The Women's Health Care Group: Mother's Magazine*. Accessed August 29, 2015. www.whcg.org/Portals/0/Mothering%20Mag%20Herbs%20and%20Pregnancy.pdf

"The Importance of Villi and the Small Intestine to the Digestion of Nutrients." Accessed August 21, 2015. *Chron*. livehealthy.chron.com/importance-villi-small-intestine-digestion-nutrients-3923.html

"Is Fermented Sourdough Bread Safe for Celiacs?" *Gluten Free Gigi*. Accessed October 2, 2015. www.glutenfreegigi.com/is-fermented-sourdough-bread-safe-for-celiacs

Kilham, Chris. "The Thyme Cure for Your Cold Symptoms." Accessed September 7, 2015. www.prevention.com/health/health-concerns/thyme-relieves-cold-symptoms

Lewis, Jessica. "The Nutritional Value of Bone Gristle." *Livestrong*. Accessed September 19, 2015. www.livestrong.com/article/545186-nutritional-value-of-bone-gristle/

"The Many Health Benefits of Raw Honey." *Dr. Axe*. Accessed September 6, 2015. draxe.com/the-many-health-benefits-of-raw-honey/

Mendes, Carly. "Nourishing Bone Broth." *Mom + Baby*. Accessed August 17, 2015. www.carleymendes.com/blog/2014/1/25/nourishing-bone-broth

Morell, Sally Fallon and Kaayla T. Daniel. *Nourishing Broth: An Old-Fashioned Remedy for the Modern World*. New York: Grand Central Life & Style, 2014.

"Natural Arthritis Diet." *Arthritis Foundation*. Accessed August 28, 2015. www.arthritis.org/living-with-arthritis/treatments/natural/

"No Bones About It." *FDA Consumer Health Information*. Accessed October 2, 2014. www.fda.gov/downloads/ForConsumers/ConsumerUpdates/UCM451245.pdf

"Potential Therapeutic Effects of Curcumin." *United States Library of Medicine*. Accessed August 29, 2015. www.ncbi.nlm.nih.gov/pmc/articles/PMC2637808/

"Stocks." The Weston. A. Price Foundation. Accessed August 29, 2015. www.westonaprice.org/health-topics/stocks/

"Ten Amazing Benefits of Eating Fat." *Poliquin Group*. Accessed August 23, 2015. www.poliquingroup.com/ArticlesMultimedia/Articles/Article/1069/Ten_Amazing_Benefits_of_Eating_Fat.aspx

Tremblay, Sylvie. "Almond Butter Benefits." *Livestrong*. Accessed September 5, 2015. www.livestrong.com/article/376742-almond-butter-benefits/

"Understanding Thyroid Problems." *Web MD*. Accessed September 3, 2015. www.webmd.com/women/guide/understanding-thyroid-problems-basics?page=2

"Villi: Function, Definition and Structure." *Study.com*. Accessed August 19, 2015. study.com/academy/lesson/villi-fucntion-definition-structure.html

Walters, Sheryl. "The Many Benefits of Coconut Oil and Coconut Butter." *Natural News*. Accessed September 6, 2015. www.naturalnews.com/023563_coconut_oil.html

Whitman, Sarah. "What are the Health Benefits of Bone Marrow." *Livestrong*. Accessed August 18, 2015. www.livestrong.com/article/445905-what-are-the-health-benefits-of-eating-bone-marrow/

"What are Probiotics? What are the Health Benefits of Probiotics?" *Medical News Today*. Accessed August 20, 2015. www.medicalnewstoday.com/articles/264721.php

Wong, Patricia. "Beef Bone Broth: A Hearty Cup of Health." *PBS*. Accessed August 20, 2015. www.pbs.org/parents/kitchenexplorers/2015/02/03/beef-bone-broth-a-hearty-cup-of-health/

Recipe Index

Index

Acknowledgments

I would like to thank all those who came before me. Those who satisfied my curiosities through years of their own work and research. Those who have paved the way on the road that has led me to this point. An extra special thanks goes out to the continuing work of the Weston A. Price Foundation and Sally Fallon.

This book is for every one of my clients at Balanced and Bright Bone Broth. You have so graciously allowed me to be a part of your lives. I cherish my relationship with every one of you.

To the professional team at Callisto Media who made writing this book a fun and fulfilling experience and who have worked tirelessly to make sure this book is not just good, but great. I would especially like to thank my editorial team—Xavier, Abigail, Katherine, and Karen—who worked around-the-clock to bring you my best work. A special round of applause goes to my managing editor Talia Platz, thank you for finding me and giving me this opportunity to share the world of bone broth with so many people, and for allowing me to be an integral part of the organic creative process in making this book great. It's been a pleasure.

Lastly, a special thanks to all of you who have been my cheerleaders when I needed it the most, picked me up when I was down, gave me ideas when I thought I had none, and most importantly never, ever let me give up on any of this. My heart will always be grateful for you: Jacquie Rimel, Carolyn Kates, Annika Decker, Julie Darling, Kim Jernigan Harris, Daniel Barron, Janella, Jon and Rowan, Hanis Cavin, Sara Stroud, Tommy Gomes, Kris Simon, Robin Fitzgerald, Logan Mitchell, Katie Saffert, Christina Ng, Alex Carballo, Catt White, Donna McLoughlin, Nitara Lockwood, and CJ and Liz Robinson.

About the Author

QUINN FARRAR WILSON owns and operates Balanced and Bright Bone Broth in San Diego, CA. After experiencing the health benefits of bone broth firsthand, Quinn set out to help others improve their health and well-being through bone broth. She frequently lectures on the health benefits of bone broth, and also works as a freelance recipe developer, culinary instructor, food stylist, and food writer. Before founding Balanced and Bright, she worked on an organic farm and developed a sustainable nutrition program for youth education. Her writing has appeared in *Edible San Diego*.

CPSIA information can be obtained
at www.ICGtesting.com
Printed in the USA
LVOW01s1724161215
466846LV00002B/2/P